Britain in the 1950s

Britain in the 1950s

Ordinary Lives in Extraordinary Times – Memories of a Post-War Decade

John Wade

PEN & SWORD HISTORY

First published in Great Britain in 2023 by
Pen & Sword History
An imprint of
Pen & Sword Books Ltd
Yorkshire – Philadelphia

ISBN 978 1 39906 138 4

Typeset by Mac Style
Printed and bound in the UK by CPI Group (UK) Ltd,
Croydon, CR0 4YY.

Pen & Sword Books Limited incorporates the imprints of Atlas,
Archaeology, Aviation, Discovery, Family History, Fiction, History,
Maritime, Military, Military Classics, Politics, Select, Transport,
True Crime, Air World, Frontline Publishing, Leo Cooper, Remember
When, Seaforth Publishing, The Praetorian Press, Wharncliffe
Local History, Wharncliffe Transport, Wharncliffe True Crime
and White Owl.

For a complete list of Pen & Sword titles please contact

PEN & SWORD BOOKS LIMITED
47 Church Street, Barnsley, South Yorkshire, S70 2AS, England
E-mail: enquiries@pen-and-sword.co.uk
Website: www.pen-and-sword.co.uk

Or

PEN AND SWORD BOOKS
1950 Lawrence Rd, Havertown, PA 19083, USA
E-mail: Uspen-and-sword@casematepublishers.com
Website: www.penandswordbooks.com

It was the best of times, it was the worst of times …
(Charles Dickens, *A Tale of Two Cities*, 1859)

The past is a foreign country; they do things differently there.
(L.P. Hartley, *The Go-Between*, 1953)

Let us be frank about it: most of our people have never had it so good.
(Prime Minister Harold Macmillan, speaking in 1957)

Contents

Timeline of the 1950s

Events and notable firsts that defined a decade

1950

January:	India severs ties with Britain and becomes a republic.
February:	*The Blue Lamp* film is released by Ealing Studios, marking the first appearance of police constable George Dixon, later to become a TV icon; BBC Television broadcasts its first election results programme; the Labour Party wins the general election.
March:	Rover tests a new turbine-powered car; *The Gambols* comic strip first appears in the *Daily Express*.
April:	Corby in Northamptonshire becomes Britain's first New Town; *Eagle* comic first appears.
May:	First package tour holiday charter takes off from Gatwick Airport; a tornado hits and tracks its way across southern England.
June:	The Korean War begins; the first organ transplant is performed in America.
August:	BBC Television makes its first broadcast from Europe.
September:	Soap rationing ends in Britain.
October:	First *Peanuts* comic strip appears in seven newspapers; a pilot episode of *The Archers* is first heard on BBC radio.
December:	Bertrand Russell wins the Nobel Prize in Literature.

1951

January:	The British Board of Film Censors introduces the X certificate rating for films deemed unsuitable for under-16s.
February:	The first commercially available computer is delivered to the University of Manchester.

March: Dennis the Menace make his first appearance in *The Beano* comic.

April: Submarine HMS *Affray* sinks, killing its crew of seventy-five; the Peak District is established as Britain's first National Park.

May: King George VI opens the Festival of Britain.

June: *The World is Yours* becomes the first regularly scheduled colour TV programme introduced in America.

August: The first Miss World beauty competition is held as part of the Festival of Britain.

October: Winston Churchill is re-elected as Prime Minister; zebra crossings are introduced on Britain's roads.

November: Express Dairies opens Britain's first full-size supermarket in London's Streatham Hill.

1952

February: King George VI dies and Princess Elizabeth becomes Queen at the age of 25; the first TV detector van is commissioned to track down people watching television without a licence; the Prime Minister announces that Britain now has an atomic bomb.

May: The de Havilland Comet becomes the word's first jet airliner.

July: Tests begin in America to find a polio vaccine; the last London tram runs.

September: The *Manchester Guardian* newspaper prints news rather than advertisements for the first time on its front page.

October: Britain explodes its first atomic bomb in Australia; tea rationing ends in Britain.

November: The first UK singles chart is published by the *New Musial Express*; *The Mousetrap* begins its epic and record-breaking run in London's West End.

December: The Great Smog engulfs London, causing thousands of deaths; the Queen makes her first Christmas speech to the Commonwealth.

1953

January:	A great flood engulfs the east coast of Britain, damaging and even demolishing many properties, killing hundreds of people.
February:	Sweet rationing ends; the DNA double-helix structure is discovered.
March:	Soviet dictator Joseph Stalin dies; Queen Mary, wife and consort of King George V, dies.
April:	*Casino Royale*, the first James Bond novel, is published; Prime Minister Winston Churchill is knighted.
May:	Mount Everest is conquered.
June:	The Coronation of Queen Elizabeth II; the first roll-on/roll-off ferry operates between Dover and Boulogne.
July:	The Korean War ends; *The Quatermass Experiment* debuts on BBC Television.
August:	The English cricket team wins The Ashes in Australia for the first time in nineteen years.
September:	Post-war rationing ends.
November:	The Danube, the first British-built nuclear weapon, is delivered to Bomber Command at RAF Wittering.
December:	Sir Winston Churchill wins the Nobel Prize in Literature; the first issue of *Playboy* is published, with Marilyn Monroe as its cover and centrefold star.

1954

January:	The first atomic submarine is launched in America; a BOAC Comet jet airliner crashes in the Mediterranean.
February:	The UK Atomic Energy Authority is founded; links between smoking and lung cancer are suggested for the first time.
April:	First field trial of polio vaccine takes place in America, involving 1.8 million children.
May:	Athlete Roger Bannister becomes the first man to run a mile in under four minutes; Diane Leather becomes the first woman to break the five-minute mile record; birth control pill trials begin.

June:	The first eclipse of the sun is seen in Britain since 1927.
August:	The maiden flight of the *English Electric Lightning*, the first supersonic aeroplane, takes place; England's first purpose-built comprehensive school opens at Greenwich in South London.
September:	The first prototype of the Routemaster bus is completed.
November:	*Fabian of the Yard*, the first police procedural television series, is premiered by the BBC.

1955

January:	The UK's first atomic bomber unit is formed at RAF Gaydon in Warwickshire.
February:	Britain suffers a big freeze across the country, which closes more than seventy roads.
April:	Poor health forces Sir Winston Churchill to resign as Prime Minister, to be replaced by Anthony Eden.
May:	The Conservatives win the general election; British Railways employees go on strike, leading to a state of emergency.
July:	Disneyland opens in California; Ruth Ellis becomes the last woman in Britain to be hanged, for shooting her lover.
August:	The Ministry of Housing and Local Government issues an invitation to local authorities to establish green belt areas; the first issue of *The Guinness Book of Records* is published.
September:	Actor James Dean dies in a car accident, age 24; Britain's first commercial TV channel is launched; Clarence Birdseye begins selling fish fingers in Britain.
November:	The Vietnam War begins.
December:	Cardiff becomes the first official capital of Wales.

1956

January:	The possession of heroin is fully criminalised.
February:	The Duke of Edinburgh's Award scheme is announced; the Routemaster bus goes into public service; double yellow no parking lines are introduced for the first time, in Slough.
March:	A memorial to Karl Marx is unveiled at London's Highgate Cemetery.

April: Premium Bonds are launched; the 2i's Coffee Bar opens in London and soon becomes a pioneering place to hear rock 'n' roll music.

May: The Gower Peninsular in South Wales becomes Britain's first designated Area of Outstanding Natural Beauty.

June: Third Class railway carriages are redesignated as Second Class.

July: The Clean Air Act is passed in response to the Great Smog of 1952; the first UK Albums Chart is published in the *Record Mirror* and is topped by *Songs for Swingin' Lovers* by Frank Sinatra; the Suez Crisis is triggered when Gamal Abdel Nasser nationalises the Suez Canal.

September: The first transatlantic telephone cable between Britain and America is inaugurated; Elvis Presley makes an early appearance on the American *Ed Sullivan Show*.

October: The Hungarian Revolution erupts against the Soviet-backed Hungarian People's Republic; Britain opens its first nuclear power station.

November: The Suez Crisis leads to petrol rationing in Britain.

December: Tea company PG Tips launches the first of its long-running television commercials featuring chimpanzees.

1957

January: Anthony Eden resigns as Prime Minister due to ill health and is succeeded by Harold Macmillan; the Cavern Club opens in Liverpool, later to be immortalised by the Beatles.

February: Norwich City Council becomes the first British local authority to install a computer; the East Midlands area of Britain suffers a mild earthquake.

March: The European Economic Community is established.

April: BBC television astronomy programme *The Sky at Night* is introduced and will run with the same presenter, Patrick Moore, until 2012.

May: Petrol rationing ends in Britain.

June: Links between smoking and lung cancer are announced; Asian Flu reaches Britain and eventually kills up to 33,000 people.

July: Paul McCartney and John Lennon meet at a church fete and will later go on to form The Beatles; Prime Minister Harold Macmillan claims, in a speech, that most people have never had it so good; the Transport and General Workers' Union stages a national strike.

August: Cartoon character Andy Capp appears for the first time in the *Daily Mirror*.

October: The Soviet satellite *Sputnik* is launched, marking the start of the space age; *Which?* magazine is first published; Jodrell Bank observatory becomes operational; plans are unveiled to allow women to join the House of Lords for the first time.

December: Wales gets its first minister of state in the Government.

1958

January: Bobby Fischer becomes the youngest chess grandmaster, age 15.

February: A plane carrying the Manchester United football team crashes on take-off in Munich, killing twenty-one of those on board, including seven players; The Campaign for Nuclear Disarmament is initiated by academic Bertrand Russell.

March: Explorer Vivian Fuchs makes the first Antarctic crossing using caterpillar tractors and a dog sleigh team; the London Planetarium opens; work begins on the M1, Britain's first full-length motorway.

April: The Church of England gives its moral backing to family planning.

June: Gatwick Airport is opened by the Queen.

July: The National Aeronautics and Space Administration (NASA) is established; parking meters are installed in Britain for the first time; the presentation of debutantes to the Royal Court is abolished.

August:	*Carry On Sergeant* becomes the first in a long line of *Carry On* films; Cliff Richard's record *Move It* is credited as being the first rock 'n' roll song produced outside America.
October:	Sovereignty of Christmas Island in the Pacific is transferred from Britain to Australia; the State Opening of Parliament is televised for the first time.
November:	British speed record-breaker Donald Campbell sets a world water speed record of 248.62 miles per hour; the world's first computer exhibition is held at London's Earl's Court exhibition centre.

1959

January:	Fidel Castro becomes Dictator of Cuba and brings communism to the Caribbean; dense fog causes chaos throughout Britain.
February:	Cyprus is granted independence from Britain.
March:	The first Barbie doll is introduced in America; The Campaign for Nuclear Disarmament attracts 20,000 demonstrators to London's Trafalgar Square.
April:	An Icelandic gunboat fires on British trawlers over fishing rights in what becomes known as the Cod War.
May:	British Empire Day is renamed British Commonwealth Day.
June:	Import tariffs are lifted in Britain; Singapore is granted self-governing status.
July:	Postcodes are introduced in Britain for the first time.
August:	The Mini car is introduced by the British Motor Corporation.
October:	Harold Macmillan is returned as Prime Minister in the general election.
November:	The first section of the M1 motorway is opened; the first duty-free shops open at Prestwick and Renfrew airports in Scotland; Britain becomes a founder member of the European Free Trade Association; *The Sound of Music* opens on Broadway and runs for 1,443 performances.

Introduction

Britain's slow recovery from the
aftermath of the Second World War

FACT BOX

- The average weekly wage in 1950 was £5 12s, rising to £8 18s by 1959.
- An average family house cost about £1,890 at the start of the decade, rising to £2,170 by the end.
- The cost of the *Daily Mirror* newspaper rose from 1d in 1950 to 2½d in 1959.
- The cost of posting a letter in Britain rose from 2½d to 3d during the decade.
- In 1951, a Murphy television with a 12-inch screen cost £80.
- Cheap ballpoint pens could be found for 1s.
- A roll of toilet paper cost about 1s 3d.
- A tin of Nescafé instant coffee cost 2s 9d.

In the 1950s, during the course of ten years, Britain went from bad times to good times, and from austerity to prosperity. The decade began less than five years after the end of the Second World War, leaving Britain strongly influenced and affected by the six years of hostilities. At the dawn of the 1950s, Britain was not a cheery place in which to live. In major cities everywhere, and particularly in London, there were still houses damaged by enemy bombs and awaiting repair. Bomb sites proliferated, heaps of rubble where once a row of houses had stood and now favourite places for young children to play. Prefabs were erected in parks and other open spaces to temporarily house those who had lost their homes. Back gardens had been turned into allotments to help feed families during the war when food was in short supply, and would be in use for a few years more. Outside of the cities, wartime military bases still stood, some abandoned, others active again in preparation for the possibility of a coming Cold War.

Taxation was high. At a time when the then current monetary system meant there were twenty shillings to a pound, the standard rate of income tax was set at nine shillings in the pound. In the early years, a shortage of manpower, food scarcity and a lack of everyday essentials were all part of daily life.

During the Second World War, the role of women changed dramatically. With the men away fighting, women stepped up to take on many of their jobs, proving themselves capable and competent in ways that neither they nor their husbands might have previously thought possible. Then the war ended, the men came home assuming they could have their old jobs back and women went back to being housewives.

Women were expected to be the homemakers, keeping the house clean and tidy, doing the washing, bringing up the children, taking them to and from school, and all the while having a hot meal ready on the table when their husbands came home from work. Women's magazines of the time, far from championing women's rights, maintained the stereotype with articles on homemaking and advertisements for all the latest household appliances aimed directly at the woman of the house, who the advertisers knew would be the driving force behind purchases of twin-tub washing machines, the latest vacuum cleaners and kitchen utensils.

There were of course exceptions, but by and large, the acceptance that a woman's place was in the home continued throughout the 1950s and well into the 1960s. And when women did work it was perfectly acceptable for them to be paid less than men, even when they were doing exactly the same job.

In the days before the Trade Descriptions Act of 1968 prevented manufacturers, retailers or service industry providers from misleading consumers, cigarettes were advertised as being essential if you wanted a good time at just about any social occasion. Eating lard was recommended for good health. Advertisements invited husbands to spank their wives for buying the wrong coffee. Equally politically incorrect advertisements suggested that what a wife really wanted for Christmas was a refrigerator and spoke about cars that were so simple to drive that even a woman could do it.

The 1950s was when children walked to school; when postmen wore uniforms with peaked hats and trousers with red stripes down the legs as they made three deliveries a day; when orange juice was free for the

According to an advertisement from 1951, cigarettes were a social necessity for enjoyment anytime, anywhere.

nation's schoolchildren; milk and bread were delivered to homes by milkmen and bakers every morning; butchers hung raw meat outside their shops on hooks; chimney sweeps rode bikes with brushes and

A NOTE ABOUT MONEY AND MEASUREMENTS

In the 1950s decimal money and metric measurements were something that few would have thought or known about. Money was calculated in pounds, shillings and pence; weights were in ounces, pounds, hundredweights and more; measurements were in inches, feet and yards. Because this was the norm throughout the decade, references in this book to money, weights, measurements and distances have been maintained in the old styles. More information on this subject will be found in the chapter on weights, measures, money and temperatures.

poles balanced on their shoulders; a local call from a telephone box cost fourpence; large towns and cities were often engulfed for days in a kind of fog called smog, popularly known as a pea-souper; and most people still seemed to prefer smooth, shiny toilet paper to the new absorbent type. Izal was one of the better-known brands responsible for this particularly uncomfortable approach to toiletry hygiene. It was not just smooth and shiny, it also smelt vaguely of disinfectant and it was used a great deal in schools, hospitals, factories and public conveniences, probably to discourage people from lingering too long in any of those locations. Much to the discomfort of many children, however, grown-ups of the early 1950s, for some unaccountable reason, also brought it into the home. It was completely unsuitable for the job in hand, although the upside for children at least, unlike the newer absorbent paper beginning to find its way onto the market, Izal was ideal for use as tracing paper.

Born from the relief of the Second World War ending, the 1950s generated a spirit of hope for the future and new beginnings. Even though the early years of the decade saw austerity and hardship, a climate gradually grew to be a comforting mixture of the traditional past blended with exciting glimpses of an exhilarating future. The following pages will explore how people lived their lives throughout this initially dreary, but ultimately exciting, decade.

Chapter 1

Life in the 1950s

*Achievements – politics – holidays – fashion –
the arrival of rock 'n' roll – the development of
household goods – the rise of brutalism*

FACT BOX

- More than half a million holidaymakers visited Butlin's holiday camps during the 1950s.
- The first package tour aeroplanes were converted from military aircraft.
- The bikini was named after the place where the first nuclear tests were carried out.
- 20 per cent of British homes owned a washing machine.
- 45 per cent of homes owned a vacuum cleaner.
- 14 per cent of homes owned a telephone.
- *White Christmas* was the best-selling record of the decade.

The first half of the 1940s had been devoured by the Second World War, and much of the second half was taken up with the recovery. The 1960s saw an opening up of society in ways that had never before been envisaged or experienced. In between stood the 1950s, a time of change and a transition from the Formal Forties to what became known as the Swinging Sixties.

After the war

Although the Second World War was over and it would be the last time enemy action would be taken against people on British soil, it was by no means the end of war for the British military called to other parts of the world.

NOTABLE ACHIEVEMENTS

The years 1950 to 1959 saw many achievements that, pre-war, would have been thought of as impossible, or had never been thought about at all. Here are some of them from Britain and around the world.

- **1950** The British-made Comet aeroplane became the world's first commercial jet airliner.
- **1951** The first credit card in general use was the American Diners Club Card, although unlike later cards, the full amount had to be paid at the end of the month. Nevertheless, 1951 saw 20,000 people sign up for the card in its first year.
- **1952** The first effective polio vaccine was developed in America by virologist and medical researcher Jonas Salk and his team at the University of Pittsburgh. It was subsequently delivered to children in Britain on sugar cubes.
- **1952** The first X-Ray picture of DNA led to the discovery of its molecular structure by British scientists James Watson and Francis Crick.
- **1953** The Conquest of Everest was made by New Zealander Edmund Hillary and the Nepalese Sherpa Tenzing Norgay. It was the first time a climb to the summit of the world's highest mountain had been achieved.
- **1954** The first organ transplant took place in America when surgeons in Massachusetts transplanted a kidney from one identical twin to another. The patient lived for eight years after the transplant.

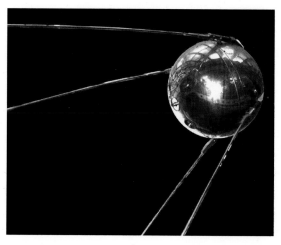

Replica of *Sputnik*, the world's first artificial satellite to be put into space.

- **1954** Athlete Roger Bannister, a 25-year-old medical student running for the Amateur Athletic Association, ran a mile in 3 minutes 59.4 seconds, thus breaking the four-minute barrier that so many before had attempted and failed to achieve.
- **1957** The Soviet Union launched, and put into orbit around the Earth, the world's first artificial satellite. It was called *Sputnik* and was about the size of a beach ball.
- **1958** Although external pacemakers had been in existence since 1950, the first internal pacemaker was invented by Doctor Åke Senning together with engineer Rune Elmqvist at the Karolinska Institute of Solna in Sweden.
- **1959** *Lunik II*, a huge Russian rocket carrying nearly 900lb of scientific instruments, successfully reached the moon, the first man-made object to do so. Its transmitters sent back much useful information before the rocket crash-landed on the moon and they ceased to operate.

At the time the Second World War ended, the Japanese had been ruling the Korean peninsula for thirty-five years. When Japan was defeated, it was decreed that Korea should be divided in two along the 38th parallel. The intention was that this would be for a five-year period culminating in independence for the unified country. The Soviet Union occupied the north, America occupied the south and the two halves began to lead very different lives, according to the influences of their occupying forces. In 1950, North Korea invaded the south in an attempt to unify the country under communist rule. The two sides called upon their allies for aid and British soldiers once again went to war. The conflict ended in 1953 with a stalemate that left the two Koreas still separated and divided by a 2½-mile wide demilitarised buffer zone.

In 1956, British troops once again found themselves involved in a foreign war following the nationalisation by Egyptian President Gamal Abdel Nasser of the Suez Canal, a waterway that controlled the traffic of two-thirds of Europe's oil. As a result, Israeli armed forces invaded Egypt, soon to be joined by French and British forces. It wasn't long before Egypt emerged victorious and the British and French withdrew troops in late 1956 and early 1957. The only real effect of the war felt by the British at home was five months of petrol rationing.

Until then, National Service had been a fact of life for boys after they left school, with all those from the ages of 17 to 21 called up to serve at least a year and half in one of the branches of the military. The system began to be phased out in 1957, with the last recruits called up in 1960.

The political climate

Britain went into the Second World War in 1939 under a Conservative government with Neville Chamberlain as Prime Minister. But it was clearly no time for party politics and, the following year, in May 1940, Chamberlain invited the Labour Party to join him in forming a coalition government. Labour leaders, however, had little faith in Chamberlain as a leader and he was forced to resign, his place as Prime Minister of the coalition government taken by Winston Churchill, previously First Lord of the Admiralty.

For many, Churchill was the voice of Britain during the war, his rousing speeches, his wit, and his talent for often verbose but always

Winston Churchill gives his famous V for Victory sign.

stirring words bringing hope and optimism to the people of Britain in their darkest hours. So when a general election was called in 1945, the year the war ended, the fact that Churchill had guided Britain through the six difficult war years, and the not unimportant fact that the Allies had won, meant that most people, Conservative politicians especially, thought it would be a forgone conclusion that Churchill would be elected at the head of a new Conservative government. It didn't happen. Instead, the Labour Party swept to power with Clement Attlee as Prime Minster. This is where things stood politically at the start of the 1950s. Then, in 1951, Attlee, in an effort to increase his majority, called another general election, only to be beaten by the Conservatives and putting Winston Churchill back in power as Prime Minster.

Britain remained under Conservative rule for the rest of the decade, with Anthony Eden replacing Churchill as Prime Minister in 1955, then Harold Macmillan taking over in 1957. In fact, Britain would remain under a Conservative government throughout the first half of the 1960s as well, with Alec Douglas-Home taking the premiership in 1963, only to be ousted by Harold Wilson, leading the Labour Party to victory in 1964. It ended what Labour Party members were keen on referring to then as 'Thirteen years of Tory misrule'.

Summer holidays

The thought of journeying abroad for a holiday at the start of the 1950s never entered the heads of most people. By the end of the decade, however, package tours to foreign climes, Spain in particular, became within the reach of many. In between came the traditional British holiday on the nearest stretch of coastline.

Seaside holidays

Few had cars at the start of the 1950s, and strangely, those that did were often loath to use them for holidays. So families were more likely to travel to their holiday destinations by train or coach. When they arrived, wealthy families might stay in hotels, but many more would stay in guest houses, in which rooms were rented out and where everyone was expected to share bathroom facilities, while meals were usually taken communally around one large table. If the service were for bed

A British Railways poster sums up the pleasures of beach holidays at Whitley Bay.

and breakfast only, many establishments expected families to leave straight after the morning meal and locked them out until early evening. Full board in some of the better guest houses provided bed, breakfast, an evening meal and even lunch as well, although frequenting rooms between meals was discouraged. Some local inhabitants of seaside towns and surrounding areas offered bed and breakfast in private homes, where guests became part of the family, sharing mealtimes and bathrooms for the duration of their stay.

Days were spent on the nearest beach, where mum and dad would sit in deckchairs, behind windbreaks if the weather was chilly, devoting time to writing postcards to friends and relatives back home. The children played on the beach, building sandcastles with their buckets and spades. These activities were interspersed with paddling and swimming in the sea,

Itinerant photographers worked along the seafronts of most seaside resorts, taking pictures with their own props.

whose tide came in and out during the course of the day, forcing those on the beach to move backwards and forwards as the day progressed. If the weather was fine, everyone enjoyed themselves. If the weather was bad, the whole experience could be gloomy, and it wasn't uncommon to see children playing on the sand under lowering skies while fully dressed in their outdoor clothes and even overcoats. When it rained, the shelters found along the promenade behind the beach would be full of shivering families, while cafés seethed with people in damp clothes huddled over pots of tea.

Not everyone had a camera to record their holiday enjoyment. But they might stop off along the seafront where photographers set up places to photograph holidaymakers with simple props like a giant teddy bear or even a live monkey. A little less professional were other photographers who roamed the seafront to take what was known as walking photographs. Photographers, both professional and semi-professional, would stalk the promenade, snapping pictures at random of passers-by and handing them tickets. Later, if those who had been photographed in this way so desired they could go along to the photographer's shop or maybe little more than a hut on the beach where the day's pictures were displayed, to present their ticket and buy a picture of themselves that had been take earlier. A lot of people happily bought the pictures, although few were very flattering to their subjects.

Caravanning holidays

During the course of the 1950s, as car ownership became more prevalent, caravanning became a popular way to take holidays. Most caravans of the time were small and cramped with rounded designs and very few windows. They were exemplified by the Berkeley Argosy, made in 1954 when its manufacturer boasted that it was the only caravan made entirely by a female workforce. The Eccles Alert was of a similar design, dating back to 1948, but continuing in production until 1955. The Eccles company had helped during the Second World War with the manufacture of specialist vehicles for the army and home front, and so had access to raw materials which gave the company a head start over most of its early rivals. The Eccles Alert was 14 feet long and slept four people, courtesy of a double bed at the front of the van and two singles at the rear, which must have filled most of the van once they had been unfolded.

A family set off for their caravan holiday in the 1950s.

One of the most luxurious vans was made by Bluebird, the largest caravan manufacturer in Britain in the 1950s. Although the company had previously specialised in static caravans, built to remain in one place on a campsite, the post-war years saw a move into the mobile caravan market, and one of the best was the Bluebird Sunparlour, first made in 1957. At 16 feet long and 7 feet wide, it was considered to be quite a beast and needed a powerful car to pull it. Many ended up being towed to campsites and left their as static vans for rental purposes. The advantage

Caravanning in the New Forest in the 1950s.

Not every campsite was glamorous in the 1950s. This one was at Crystal Palace in London.

over other static vans was that the Sunparlour was a lot more mobile and easier to transport to a campsite than many of its type. The makers, however, advertised it as a mobile model with the slogan, 'Follow the sun with the Sunparlour.'

When caravanners arrived at their holiday destinations, some parked for a week or more where they could, often in farmers' fields. Others stayed on recognised campsites, situated near beaches and on clifftops, in which rows and rows of caravans were situated in regimental formation.

Farm holidays

In some areas of the country, Kent in particular, families might spend their holidays on farms sleeping in huts at night and occupying their days picking hops, which were used to make beer. This was in the days before mechanisation, when farmers needed the extra labour at certain times of the year. It was hard work, but many saw it as a chance to earn some extra cash while getting away from the towns and cities to spend

Hop picking in Kent.

a pleasant time in the countryside. The hop picking season fell around September.

Holiday camps

Holiday camps were another destination for the holidaymaker in the 1950s, and Butlin's was the most famous. The camps were created by Billy Butlin, a South African-born British entrepreneur who bought land and opened his first holiday camp at Skegness in 1936. His ambition was to give holidaymakers, all in one place, accommodation in basic yet comfortable chalets, daily amusements, competitions, fairground rides, swimming pools and decent food served in large communal dining rooms, all at affordable prices. One objective was for all guests to mingle

Getting around at a Butlin's Holiday Camp in the 1950s.

and enjoy one another's company, rather than just mixing with their own family units. He also wanted to make families feel they were being looked after during every minute of their stay. With that in mind, very early in the history of the camps, Butlin built a team of people who were more than just staff members. Their purpose was to mix with families, make friends with them, tell jokes and generally encourage them to have a good time with other guests. The team all wore red blazers and became known as Redcoats.

Two years after his first camp opened in Skegness, Butlin chose Clacton for a second camp. When the Second World War broke out in 1939, the camps were given over to the Government for army accommodation. When the war ended in 1945, Butlin bought them back and, throughout the 1950s, opened new camps all across Britain. To quote Butlin's own publicity material: 'The integration of the Butlin Camps into the life fabric of the peoples of this island is a social phenomenon of our time.' In the 1950s, more than half a million holidaymakers passed through the Butlin camps during every season.

Butlin's provided a wealth of entertainment for families within each camp.

The dining room at Butlin's Skegness holiday camp in the 1950s.

Even though the camps were mostly situated in well-known coastal seaside resorts, many who booked in for a week or two-week holiday in the 1950s never left the environment of the camp during their stay. Everything they needed to have a good time was right there, all in one place, all day long.

Package holidays

Despite the majority of people staying at home for their holidays at this time, the decade did, nevertheless, mark the start of package tour holidays, in which flights, accommodation, food and other necessities were all combined into a single cost. Although the Thomas Cook travel company had pioneered organised tours by train as far back as 1841 and continued to promote foreign holidays in the early 1950s, it was the Horizon Holiday Group that introduced the first package holidays for the British to travel abroad. The company was co-founded by Russian-born entrepreneur Vladimir Raitz. Holidaying in Corsica in 1949, he found himself being asked to encourage British holidaymakers to visit the island. He was in the right place at the right time. With the Second World War over, but Britain still in a somewhat dreary state, a small number of people began looking at the possibility of foreign travel, if only it could be attained at a reasonable price. Raitz set up the Horizon Holiday Group, the name chosen to reflect the blue horizon passengers would see from aircraft windows. With the company established, he began to look into how he could charter planes and tie the flights in with transfers to hotels

A DC3 Dakota that was converted for passenger use during the first holiday package tours.

all in a single package that would cost less than £35. His first flights were from Gatwick Airport in West Sussex to Corsica in 1950, followed by Palma in 1952 and Lourdes in 1953.

The first flight from Gatwick to Corsica was in a DC3 Dakota plane, converted from military use to carry thirty-two passengers. Most of the passengers were teachers and students who had responded to advertisements in the *Nursing Mirror* and *New Statesman*. At that time, British European Airways (BEA) was charging £70 for a trip from London to Nice in Southern France. Raitz brought in his package tour to Corsica, including flight, transfers and the hotel, for just £32. Although only 7 per cent of British people travelled abroad for their holidays in the early 1950s, the British package holiday business began to take off and, by the end of the decade, had become a popular and acceptable way to take holidays.

Fashion

With a new decade came new fashions for both men and women, all of which continued to evolve throughout the 1950s.

Women

Ladies' fashions brought a new glamour to the austerity of the 1950s, as women and girls sought to dress and style their hair in shorter cuts than previously, adopting hairstyles that aspired to copy film stars of the day like Audrey Hepburn. In an age when there was nothing incorrect about wearing fur, most women wanted a fur coat, and a mink coat was the most coveted of all. It was a time when girls stopped dressing like their mothers and began to buy clothes that represented a new youthful look.

French designer Christian Dior took women's fashion away from the rather staid previous years and introduced what became known as the New Look. His designs defied the climate of rationing by using far more material in his garments than some thought strictly necessary. The result was calf-length dresses with narrow waists and wide skirts. As Dior continued to dominate fashion throughout the 1950s, he introduced the Princess Line in 1953, which used long panels along the length of a dress without a horizontal join or separation at the waist. In 1955, he produced the A-line, which was applied to both skirts and dresses with a design

High fashion comes to the high street in a Pontins clothing catalogue for 1958.

that gradually widened towards the hem, like the shape of a letter 'A'. Dior's biggest rival was Coco Chanel, famous for her women's suit, which featured a collarless jacket teamed with a skirt that finished just below the knee.

Both the original Dior and Chanel garments were aimed at the rich, but it wasn't long after their arrival on the catwalks before they were copied by British high-street shops, selling far less expensive examples of the styles. Jumpers and trousers became popular during the decade, with women's trousers similar in style to men's garments but with narrower legs and tighter fits. Jeans also began to be popular for casual wear.

When it came to swimwear, the latest fashion for women was the bikini. The daring two-piece swimsuit was first shown in 1946 by French motor engineer turned clothing designer Louis Réard. Following the end

French actress Brigitte Bardot helps popularise the bikini in 1953.

of the Second World War, it was a time when material for making dresses and the like was still in short supply, which was one way of justifying the fact that Monsieur Réard's design used no more than four triangles of cloth. He named it the bikini, after the Bikini Atoll, a group of islands in the Pacific Ocean where America conducted its first nuclear tests. He thought his new swimsuit style might be as explosive as an atom bomb. In fact, the bikini was considered outrageous by many and Réard could not find a professional fashion model to demonstrate its charms. In the end, he called on the services of a nightclub dancer to model the bikini at a swimwear event. The press went crazy and the dancer received more than 50,000 fan letters.

Despite the fact that beaches in Spain, Portugal, France and Australia at first banned the bikini, the 1950s saw a rise in its popularity and its acceptance as something that could be decently worn in public. The bikini's reputation was helped by actresses that included Elizabeth Taylor, Jayne Mansfield and Marilyn Monroe in America as well as Brigitte Bardot in France posing in bikinis while, in Britain, actress and singer Diana Dors did nothing to harm her image as the British Blonde Bombshell when she wore a mink bikini at the Venice Film Festival in 1955.

The swimwear was immortalised in music by singer Brian Hyland in 1960 when he recorded a pop song called 'Itsy Bitsy Teenie Weenie Yellow Polka-Dot Bikini'. It reached number eight in the music charts.

Men

Fashions for men during the 1950s differed little from the pre-war years, with conservative suits, often made to measure by shops like Montague Burton. Ties were always worn with such suits. Sports jackets and blazers with open-neck shirts whose collars were folded outside the jacket were for more casual occasions. At least that was the case for the middle-age and old-age men.

For young men a new youth cult arrived in the 1950s. Initially it spread only among the wealthy upper classes, whose youth fought against the drab austere look of post-war Britain by dressing more like their Edwardian ancestors of forty years before. From this, working-class boys and young men created their own less expensive and therefore more accessible look. They became known as Teddy Boys. Also more simply known as Teds, they wore long jackets of plain material often coloured grey or blue, with velvet collars. Trousers were ultra-slim, tight-fitting and referred to as

Lounge Suits

The beauty of ready-to-wear is that you

can see the suit on and satisfy

yourself as to fit, colour,

pattern, cloth, before you buy.

MOSS BROS & CO. LTD.
OF COVENT GARDEN
THE COMPLETE MAN'S STORE

Junction of Garrick and Bedford Streets, W.C.2 *Temple Bar 4477*
AND BRANCHES

A 1951 Moss Bros advertisement shows men were conservative in the way they aspired to dress.

drainpipes. Ties also were narrow, sometimes with horizontal stripes, alternated with American bootlace style ties. Shoes had thick crepe soles and were sometimes called brothel creepers.

Teds also had their own hairstyle, longer than before with plenty of hair cream to produce a large quiff at the front, which was sometimes so exaggerated that it became almost like a sausage shape. At the back, the hair was combed from each side to meet in the middle and then a comb used to introduce a parting from the crown of the head to the nape of the neck. The style was known politely as a ducktail, but more commonly as a DA, in which the 'D' stood for 'duck' and the 'A' stood for a rather more vulgar name referring to the bird's rear end.

The Teddy Boy style was very smart. There were stories of Teddy Boy gangs politely helping out in the community, but unfortunately the cult was more commonly associated with violence, sometimes clashing with immigrants to Britain, but also for fights between rival Teddy Boy gangs. It was said that they carried cut-throat razors and bicycle chains for use as weapons. When rock 'n' roll music arrived in the mid-1950s, the Teds adopted it as their anthem and violence could easily become part of the way they danced to the music.

The traditional drape jacket style of the Teddy Boys.

In the home

Plan your dream kitchen with Hygena units. You can buy them all in one wonderful day—or unit by unit if you're tied to a limited budget. A Hygena kitchen is every woman's dream—crisp, compact units, each one with a colourful wipe-clean Formica working top, each one finished in brilliant, durable high gloss enamel. We have been planning kitchens for more than thirty years. Reliable construction, practical design and fastidious attention to detail are second nature to Hygena.

Start living with Hygena —and see your dreams come true. The wide variety of Hygena units gives you unlimited scope in planning your own ideal kitchen.

Start living with a **Hygena** KITCHENE

Fitted kitchens from manufacturers like Hygena began to appear in the 1950s.

Homes at the start of the 1950s were not equipped with many appliances. Although fitted kitchens began to make an appearance during the decade, the kitchen in the average house contained not much more than a sink and draining board with various mismatched cupboards. Hot water over the sink often came from a geyser, a gas-driven device which sprung into life as its tap was turned, using a miniature boiler to heat cold water that entered from one end and was dispensed as hot water at the other end. Hot water for kitchens and bathrooms was also supplied by a back burner, a water tank situated behind the coal fire in a house's living room.

Many kitchens contained wooden larder cabinets. These were tall pieces of furniture that contained various cupboards, drawers and fold-down work surfaces.

In the mid-1950s, only 20 per cent of British homes had washing machines. It was far more likely that a housewife (and it was the wife, not the husband) washed clothes by hand and hung them out to dry on a clothesline that ran the length of the garden. Monday was washing day in most households. Those that did own a washing machine were likely to be using something like a Servis, advertised as 'The washer that has everything.' Standing 32 inches high and 20 inches square, the Servis comprised a tank that was connected to the water mains or more simply to a kitchen tap to fill it with water. At the base there was an electric heating element to boil the water and a contraption that the Servis company called a Turbulator. With the washing in the water, the heater bringing it to the boil and suitable washing powder added, the Turbulator rotated back and forth to stir up the water and the clothes in what Servis referred to as an offset vortex action. When it was considered they had been washed enough, the clothes were removed and put through a small hand-operated mangle or wringer that sat on the top of the machine.

Much more expensive twin tub washing machines also made an appearance in the 1950s. As the name implied, each machine had two tubs, one for washing the clothes, the other beside it for spinning and drying.

For many families of the 1950s, kitchen larder cabinets were more common than fitted kitchens.

With no washing machine, clothes, sheets and any other washing were hand washed and hung out to dry on a clothesline in the garden.

A Servis advertisement illustrates the simplicity of using a 1950s washing machine.

Progress in the Home

Hoover Limited take pride in the fact that their products are saving millions of housewives from hard, wearisome drudgery — not only in Britain but throughout the world. Wherever the name Hoover appears it is a guarantee of excellence.

THE WORLD-FAMOUS HOOVER CLEANER

The Hoover Cleaner, with its famous triple-action principle — " It beats . . . as it sweeps . . . as it cleans " — is undeniably the world's best cleaner — best in design, best in materials, best in quality of workmanship. There is a model suitable for every size and type of home.

THE MARVELLOUS HOOVER ELECTRIC WASHING MACHINE

The Hoover Electric Washing Machine has completely revolutionised the whole conception of washing-day in the home. It does the full weekly wash for a large family and yet is such a handy size—suitable for even the smallest kitchen.

VISIT THE HOOVER FACTORY

Visitors to the Festival of Britain are cordially invited to make a tour of the Hoover Factories at Perivale, Middlesex, or Merthyr Tydfil, South Wales, or Cambuslang, Scotland. Please write to, Hoover Limited, Perivale, or 'phone Perivale 3311 for more information.

HOOVER LIMITED

Factories at :

PERIVALE, MIDDLESEX · MERTHYR TYDFIL · HIGH WYCOMBE · CAMBUSLANG, SCOTLAND

The Hoover company supplied both washing machines and vacuum cleaners.

Washing machine ownership increased to 40 per cent by the end of the 1950s. Those who never aspired to own one often took their clothes to the local launderette. Found in many high streets, these were shops that had been converted to hold coin-operated washing machines and spin dryers.

Forty-five per cent of British homes owned a vacuum cleaner in the 1950s. They took two forms. One was upright, with a handle attached to the cleaning mechanism that sucked dust and dirt off the floor and into a bag on the front that hung from the handle. The second type was horizontal, consisting of a long tube that contained the motor and bag and to which various attachments were fitted to clean floors as well as curtains and upholstery. Anyone that didn't own a vacuum cleaner was likely to have had a carpet sweeper which consisted of a box on wheels with a broom handle attached. Brushes inside the box rotated and swept dust into a container as the handle was used to push the device across the floor.

Only 14 per cent of 1950s homes owned a telephone. They were operated by a branch of the General Post Office throughout Britain, with the exception of Hull, which had its own telephone service. The cost of installing a telephone was £5 with a quarterly bill of £3, which allowed 100 free calls a year. At first, the phones did not have dials or any other method of calling a number. Instead, the user picked up the receiver and waited for the operator to enquire 'Number please?' Once the number of the person to be called had been given, the operator made the connection manually. There were two types of call. Local calls, which were from one person to another within the local exchange area, allowed the caller to remain on the phone as long as he or she liked. Trunk calls that connected phone users over greater distances were charged in increments of three minutes, according to the number of miles between the caller and the person being called. They ranged from 8*d* for between 15 and 25 miles to 1*s* 6*d* for distances of more than 25 miles.

Not long into the decade dials appeared on British telephones, allowing users to dial in the name of the exchange, usually abbreviated to three letters indicated on the dial along with the numbers, followed by the

An early British dial telephone. The button above the dial was used to indicate to the exchange who on a shared line wanted to make a call.

number. It was not unusual, even then, for those with private, rather than business, phones to share their line with another phone owner nearby. Before speaking to the operator, it was necessary to press a button on the phone to indicate who needed to use the line. If the line was already in use by the other person who shared it, then their conversation could be overheard. In those circumstances it was polite to hang up and try again later, though it was always tempting to listen in on a neighbour's conversation.

Back in the kitchen, domestic refrigerators began to make their first appearances during the 1950s, although only around 10 per cent of homes owned one at the start of the decade, a figure that doubled by the end.

Music

One of the best-selling records of all time was on sale throughout most of the 1950s. It was called 'White Christmas'. The song was originally heard in a 1942 film called *Holiday Inn*, starring Bing Crosby with Fred Astaire. It was heard again in another film, actually called *White Christmas*, in 1954, again starring Big Crosby, this time with Danny Kaye. The song was written by Irving Berlin and it sold 20 million copies, of which 10 million were attributed to Bing Crosby. The song was typical of the sentimental ballad popularised by singers like Perry Como and Frankie Laine and heard regularly during the first half of the 1950s. And then, in 1955, rock 'n' roll arrived.

This new music, far more brash than much of what had been heard before, reached Britain courtesy of an American film called *Blackboard Jungle*. It concerned a school where teenage lawlessness had broken out and the song that typified the plot was 'Rock Around The Clock', belted out by Bill Haley and the Comets over the final credits. Almost overnight a new youth culture was born, widely condemned by older generations.

Meanwhile, skiffle groups began to appear, mostly among amateur and aspiring professional musicians. The music was a mixture of folk, blues and jazz, performed by small groups with a guitar alongside home-made instruments. One was made by attaching a broom handle to a tea chest and stretching a piece of stout string from the top of the handle to the centre of the chest. Keeping the string taught, this was plucked to produce a regular deep base note sound. Percussion came courtesy of

Bill Haley and the Comets bring rock 'n' roll to a new generation of music fans.

a washing board made of a piece of heavy ribbed glass set in a wooden frame. Its real job was for rubbing soapy clothes on the ribbed glass to clean them. In the skiffle world, the ribbed glass was stroked and tapped by the musicians with thimbles on their fingers. One of the few musicians to take skiffle into the professional world was Lonnie Donegan, who had a couple of hits with the style of music in 1956.

Rock 'n' roll and skiffle tended to be considered working class and were looked down upon by middle-class music fans who preferred modern jazz. A typical jazz combo of the time comprised a pianist, bass player, drummer and one other who played a brass instrument such as a saxophone. Modern jazz took popular and well-known tunes with each member of the group improvising their own versions of the melody, often straying a long way from the original. The music was chiefly performed in jazz clubs.

Despite these various types of music gaining in popularity throughout the 1950s, the core of the record-buying public still went for the more traditional ballads. In 1955, Bill Hayley and the Comets were the best sellers with 'Rock Around The Clock'. But the following years saw more traditional artists taking the best-selling spots. They included Johnnie Ray singing 'Just Walkin' in the Rain' (1956), Paul Anka singing 'Diana' (1957), Perry Como singing 'Magic Moments' (1958) and Cliff Richard and the Drifters singing 'Living Doll' (1959).

Houses and architecture

Following the Second World War, the shortage of building materials, coupled with the number of houses that had been destroyed in bombing raids, led to a severe lack of homes. One short-term solution was the erection of prefabricated houses, popularly known as prefabs. Several types were planned including a timber-framed design, another with steel frames and asbestos panels, and a third made of aluminium from surplus aircraft materials. They were one-storey buildings, sometimes detached, sometimes erected in terraces, and they could be built by workers with a minimum of experience who erected them quickly in places like parks and wasteland. Between the end of the war in 1945 and 1955, an estimated 1.5 million prefabs were built, each with an expected life of ten years. In fact, they remained standing and occupied for a lot longer.

During the course of the 1950s, house building progressed and peaked. Because of the high demand, houses that were cheap and easy to construct

A 1950s prefab, preserved today at St Fagans National Museum of History in Wales.

became the main requirement. The result was a period of houses made from reinforced concrete panels bolted onto steel frames.

Naturally, not every house in Britain had been destroyed in the war and there still remained streets of detached, semi-detached and terraced houses, the last of which meant all the homes in the street were joined together, usually with an entrance to an alley at regular intervals. These led down the side and round the back of the rows of houses, giving access to small back gardens and were used frequently by council workers who arrived each week to empty dustbins left for them at the end of the gardens. In poorer areas, many of these terraced homes contained no more than two rooms downstairs with an attached scullery and two rooms upstairs accessed by staircases ascending in the centre of the houses. They were known as 'two-ups, two-downs'. Toilets were invariably outside the house.

During the decade, many of these older types of houses were cleared away under a slum clearance plan that enabled local councils to control the purchase of land for housing developments. They were often replaced with what became known as 'streets in the sky'. In reality, they were tower blocks of flats, cheap to buy and easy to build from prefabricated materials, and since the Government provided subsidies for any blocks higher than six storeys, builders were incentivised to build higher and higher blocks.

Unfortunately, the tower blocks were rarely well constructed, needing constant repair and maintenance. By the end of the decade and the early years of the next, what had at first seemed to be the height of modernity rapidly became worse slums than the houses they had replaced, the major difference being that rather than housing people side by side, they housed their occupants one on top of another.

All of this paints a rather gloomy picture of government and council involvement in rehousing post-war British people. In fact, the other side of this particular coin was illustrated more successfully with the decade's period of council house building. These houses, allocated to the most deserving according to their financial state and their positions on housing lists, were far more attractive than the sometimes misplaced conception of convenience housing that had resulted in prefabs and tower blocks. Although the architectural styles of most council houses were usually boxlike and not particularly attractive, they were sometimes built on greenfield sites, with good sized gardens. Council houses were utilitarian, provided more than adequate accommodation for deserving families and were much sought-after by many.

As the decade progressed, and austerity turned to prosperity, a new generation of home owners emerged, thanks to cheaper housing. At the same time, houses took on new and, according to some, rather more daring aspects, as architects experimented with different designs and often unconventional interiors. Tall town houses with two floors, rather than one, above the ground floor began to be popular. Lounges, which had always been traditionally on the ground floor, started appearing on top floors. Outside toilets, still very much a feature of houses left over from the Victorian era, came indoors and moved upstairs side by side with bathrooms.

A lot of this new type of housing was built following the 1946 New Towns Act, which established an ambitious plan for building New Towns around the country, to accommodate people who had lost their homes during the war and had become an overspill population from major cities, primarily London. Most of the new towns took on the names of smaller communities nearby. The first was Stevenage in Hertfordshire, which received much of its population from North London. Ten other New Towns had been built around the country by 1955.

Housing at Stevenage, Hertfordshire, epitomises the new kind of housing that sprung up in the New Towns during the 1950s.

The New Towns consisted of complete communities with major shops of the day, all the amenities required to support a new population and of course the houses, built on estates with wide roads and often close to green fields. They were a long way removed from the back streets of cities like London from where the population had migrated. The New Towns of the 1950s still survive today. Although the style of their houses looks dated and in some areas dilapidated, they stand as a testimony to the vision of a new Britain that emerged after the Second World War and so much characterised the 1950s.

The construction of public buildings too began to take on a new and more modern aspect. The Royal Festival Hall, on the south bank of the river Thames, was a perfect example of the new modernism. Built as part of the 1951 Festival exhibition, but also destined to remain long after the exhibition had been forgotten, its ultra-modern design was summed up perfectly in the official Festival Exhibition brochure:

> The simplicity of the external design of the Hall may give little hint of the care and skill which have gone into every detail of its construction. This has resulted not only in good acoustics, but also in the greatest comfort for audience and players. Innovations include the double-skinned wall, designed to exclude noise, and the tuning of the concert hall auditorium after the building work had been completed. The

The Royal Festival Hall as it is today.

concert hall holds an audience of 3,300. There is also provision for an orchestra of more than 100 and a choir of 250. In addition, the Royal Festival Hall can claim to be a work of art in itself. The superb dramatic effects of space and vista, within the building and beyond it to the river and the city, are things which the visitor will discover for himself.

Practically side by side with where the Royal Festival Hall stands today, another building of a much more radical design demonstrates an emerging style of architecture from the 1950s. Although opened, after many delays, in 1976, the design of the Royal National Theatre lies in a movement that began and became popular in the 1950s. It was called Brutalism.

Brutalist architecture was characterised by minimalist designs that often showed bare and unpainted building materials like concrete or

The Brutalist style of architecture stands in stark contrast to the older terraced house that surrounded the Balfron Tower block of flats in East London.

brick in starkly geometric shapes with modular designs that represented different functioning zones of the building. A building's inner workings – such as lift shafts – were sometimes incorporated into the exterior of the buildings rather than the traditional style of hiding them away inside. Wood, glass and steel were also incorporated in designs. Apart from prestigious buildings like the National Theatre, the 1950s saw Brutalism employed in utilitarian, low-cost social housing that included blocks of high-rise flats, along with buildings such as university facilities, car parks, leisure centres and libraries.

The Brutalist design movement, which originated in post-war Britain, spread around the world and remained popular through the 1960s and into the 1970s. The style still has its fans, even though Brutalism emerged at a time when architecture, in the minds of many, attained new peaks of ugliness.

Chapter 2

Measure for Measure

Money – weights – distances – temperatures

FACT BOX

- Pre-decimal currency was measured in pounds, shillings and pence.
- Pounds, shillings and pence were designated as LSD, reflecting their Latin origins.
- The word 'pound' was used for money and weight because, originally, one pound weight of silver was worth one monetary pound.
- A pound weight was abbreviated to 'lb', relating to the Latin words 'libra pondo'.
- Originally, zero degrees referred to boiling point and 100 degrees indicated freezing point.
- Units of weight and distance once included the clove, tod, sack, rod, pole, perch and link.

L iving in today's world of decimal money and metric measurements, all based on the idea that everything is basically a multiple of ten, it seems impossible that money, weights and measures in the 1950s relied on learning that the units used for each system divided into each other using what appeared to be a senseless group of non-related random numbers. There were, for example, 240 pennies in a pound; 16 ounces in a different kind of pound; 22 yards to a chain, 10 chains to a furlong and 8 furlongs to a mile.

Money

Unlike today's system of two monetary units where a pound is quite simply made up of 100 pence, the monetary system of the 1950s was based on three units: pounds, shillings and pence. To make things more confusing, these three units were not abbreviated, as might be expected, to PSP, but to LSD. To make matters even more confusing, the 'L' was stylised (as it remains today) to make the '£' symbol.

To understand how this confusing system came about, it's necessary to go back to Ancient Rome, and to remember that the word 'pound' doesn't just refer to money; it is also a unit of weight. The Roman monetary system consisted of libri, solidi and denarii. One librus (the singular term for libri) was made from 1 pound weight of silver, from which 240 denarii were minted. There were twelve denarii to a solidus (the singular term for solidi) and twenty solidi to one librus. In the eighth century this system was simplified in Western Europe by removing the solidi units and just using libri and denarii. When the libri and denarii system reached the British Isles, King Offa of Mercia introduced silver pennies or sterlings, 240 of which were minted from 1 pound of silver. So now British currency consisted of pounds and sterlings, or pennies. Then, in the eleventh century, shillings were incorporated into the monetary system and, like the solidi of Ancient Rome, it was decided that there should be twenty shillings to the pound, which meant there had to be twelve pennies to the shilling. Although these units were known in Britain as pounds, shillings and pennies, Latin being the language of law and record in Medieval England, the three units were abbreviated, according to their Roman names libri, solidi and denarii, to LSD.

Fast forward, then, to the 1950s, by which time the word 'sterling' was still in use with the word 'pound', as in 'pounds sterling' to refer to British currency, although it had now been replaced in the coinage system with the word 'penny', which in itself was interchangeable with the word 'pence', according to context.

So, just to recap, there were twelve pennies to the shilling and twenty shillings to the pound, and while people in the 1950s spoke about prices in pounds, shillings and pence, they wrote prices down in terms of LSD. A price spoken of as nine pounds, eleven shillings and five pence, for example, would be written as £9 11s 5d. In everyday conversation, units other than the pound were rarely mentioned. So, when speaking about that same price of £9 11s 5d, the speaker would say, 'nine pounds, eleven and five'. Similarly, with prices of less than a pound, what was written as 3s 6d would be described as 'three and six'. Also, although everyone knew

Notes in circulation during the 1950s: a rarely seen £5 note (often known as a white fiver), ten-shilling note and pound note.

they had penny coins in their pockets, the word became 'pence' when speaking of a price. No one would say something cost ten pennies, they would say it cost tenpence.

There were coins for everything up to a pound, then paper notes took over. Half way to a pound, however, there was also a paper ten-shilling note. Rarely seen in those days, a five-pound note was printed on white paper and about the size of four one-pound or ten-shilling notes. The smallest coin was a farthing, which was a quarter of a penny, and there were two of these to a ha'penny, which was worth half a penny. There was a small twelve-sided coin worth three pennies and generally known as threepence, thruppence, or – most commonly – a thruppenny bit. A coin that was worth six pennies was known as a sixpence. There was of course a shilling coin, worth twelve pennies, but there was also a two-shilling coin, known as a florin. Surprisingly, there was also a coin worth just sixpence more, valued at 2s 6d. That one was known as half a crown because two of them made a crown, which was the coinage name for five shillings. Five-pound coins, however, had died out, except for special versions minted for occasions, such as the Queen's Coronation in 1953.

Coins up to 100 years old or even more were still in use, and it wasn't unusual to find extremely well-worn pennies dating back to the early Victorian age in everyday circulation. Gold sovereigns, nominally worth £1, but actually worth more on the collector's market, were still around, but rarely used commercially. One other term, still in use in the 1950s, was the guinea. There was no guinea coin or note, it was just a term used to define the sum of £1 1*s*. Professional bodies, especially those involved with the law, usually charged their fees in guineas.

Pity the poor schoolboy or schoolgirl of the 1950s who had to learn how to add up pounds, shillings and pence as part of their arithmetic lessons. First the pence column was added up. If the answer came to more than twelve, then that number was divided by twelve. The whole number was taken over to the shillings column and the remaining figure, or remainder, was placed in the pence total. Then the shillings column was added up, along with the figure taken over from the pence column. If this figure was greater than twenty, then it was divided by twenty and, once again, the whole number was taken over to the pounds column and the remainder placed in the shillings total. The last number taken over from the shillings column was then added along with the numbers in the pounds column and that total was placed in the pounds total. The resulting figure was the sum in pounds, shillings and pence. Having pitied those who had to learn this system, have some admiration for grocers, greengrocers, market traders and many more shopkeepers who could add it all up in their heads.

And then there was the slang. Five shillings, of which there were four to the pound, was often referred to as a dollar, stemming from the Second World War when many British people fraternised for the first time with Americans when there were roughly four dollars to the pound. Everyone in the 1950s knew that a sixpence coin was a tanner, a shilling was a bob and a pound was a nicker, a quid, or sometimes a sov. Strangely, the first two slang terms were never referred to in the plural. Something might cost five bob, never five bobs; and something more expensive might cost three quid or three nicker, never three quids or three nickers. The sov, a term derived from the sovereign, however, was spoken about in the plural, as in, 'that coat cost me twenty sovs'. A ten-shilling note was of

Woolworth shop assistants line up behind a counter full of Easter goods priced in shillings and pence during spring 1951.

course a ten-bob note, while anything that cost £5 or £10 was known to cost a fiver or a tenner. Shillings and pence prices in shops were often displayed as numbers with what is today known as a slash between the figures. So five shillings and sixpence, for example, would be displayed as 5/6. If the price was in shillings only, the lack of pence was displayed as a dash: three shillings, for example, was displayed as 3/-.

There was also the strange practice of referring to things that cost just a little more than a pound, in terms only of shillings. In that way, £1 10s became thirty bob, and £2 10s became fifty bob. In a similar way, 1s 6d was often referred to as eighteen pence. There were also slang terms for higher amounts of currency that the average man or woman wouldn't have cause to use, simply because they rarely handled that kind of cash. So £1,000 was a grand, £500 was a monkey, £100 was a ton, £25 was a pony and £20 was a score.

Some of these terms, especially those that refer to multiples of a pound, still survive today, the most notable of which is a grand for £1,000. The vast majority of these old terms, however, vanished for ever when Britain adopted decimal currency on 15 February 1971.

Weights

If schoolchildren of the 1950s were to be pitied for having to learn a difficult monetary system, things got even worse when they began to learn about weights. The system was similarly divided into units with no immediately obvious reason for the numbers of units that made up the next one up the scale. Also, just like the initially confusing methods of writing pounds, shillings and pence, abbreviations for some of the most common weights were equally confusing. So why was 'ounce' or 'ounces' abbreviated to 'oz', when there was no 'z' in either word? Why would 'pound' or 'pounds' be abbreviated to 'lb'? Once again, it all goes back to the Romans.

In Latin, the primary meanings for the word 'libra' were 'balance' or 'scales'. That's why scales are still used to symbolise the star sign Libra. The word was also used in a unit of measure called the 'libra pondo', which meant 'a pound by weight'. In English, the word 'pound', when it applies to weight rather than money, comes from the 'pondo' part, while the 'lb' abbreviation for a pound weight comes from the 'libra' part. The reason why 'ounce' or 'ounces' became abbreviated to 'oz' is a little more

Scales typical of the 1950s, with weights of 1lb, 8oz, 4oz, 2oz, ½oz and ¼oz.

convoluted. It starts with the word 'uncia', which was the Roman name for an ounce in weight terms, or an inch in terms of measurement. By the time that word reached medieval Italian, it had become 'onza', from which the English language took 'oz' as the abbreviation. The abbreviation for the hundredweight is a little more straightforward. It derives from the fact that the measurement of weight was once known as a centum weight, and so went on to be abbreviated to 'cwt'.

The rest of the strange British way of measuring weights was simpler, as far as abbreviations were concerned, but just as complicated when it came to understanding how much of what went into which. The basics that everyone had to learn at school were these …

16oz = 1lb
14lb = 1 stone
2 stones = 1 quarter
4 quarters = 1cwt
20cwt = 1 ton

For those who wanted to be more precise there were also all kinds of odd terms for weights that were multiples of the pound. They went like this …

7lb = 1 clove
28lb = 1 tod
112lb = 1cwt
364lb = 1 sack
2,240lb = 1 ton

What we're dealing with here of course is Britain in the 1950s, but it is maybe worth mentioning that in America things were seen a little differently. In the US, there were 100 pounds to the hundredweight, while in Britain there were 112 pounds to the hundredweight. Because there were still 20 hundredweights to 1 ton, irrespective of how many pounds each contained, an American ton was equivalent to 2,000 pounds while a British ton was equivalent to 2,240 pounds.

Officially, Britain adopted the metric system in 1965, but the changeover wasn't as instant as it had to be with money. For many years following, no one bothered to make the change, with shops continuing to sell goods in pounds and ounces and people defining their weights in stones and pounds.

Temperature

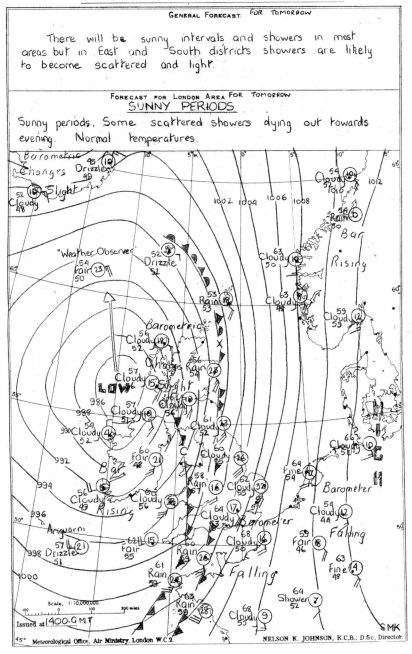

A daily weather forecast issued by the Meteorological Office and available at the Festival Exhibition in 1951 designated temperatures in Fahrenheit.

Anyone setting out to design a scale of temperatures starting with the freezing point of water and rising to its boiling point, might find it obvious to start with 0 degrees at the lower end of the scale and 100 degrees at the top. Not so in Britain of the 1950s, when freezing point was designated as 32 degrees and boiling point as 212 degrees.

This was because temperature in the 1950s (and for more than 200 years before) was measured on the Fahrenheit scale, which was formulated in 1724 by German physicist Daniel Gabriel Fahrenheit. He placed the lower end of his scale as the temperature of an equal mixture of ice and salt and assigned this the value of 30 degrees. He then designated normal body temperature as 90 degrees. These figures were later adjusted to 32 degrees and 96 degrees, with the latter finally being adjusted to 98.6 degrees. The boiling point of water then became 212 degrees. Quite why the physicist chose these delineations is largely unknown.

In 1742, Swedish physicist Anders Celsius invented a new temperature scale that put 0 degrees as the boiling pint of water and 100 degrees as its freezing point. It became known as the Celsius scale, or the Centigrade scale, since the definition of the word 'centigrade' is something that is divided into 100 degrees. This scale was later inverted to put 0 degrees at the bottom and 100 degrees at the top.

Despite the fact that Europe adopted the Celsius scale, Britain resisted and throughout the 1950s just about everyone referred to temperatures in terms of the Fahrenheit scale. The habit continued for many years even though the Meteorological Office converted weather forecasts to Celsius/Centigrade in 1962.

Measurements

Although Britain today has largely adopted the metric system for measuring size, it's rather incongruous that the old imperial system is still retained for measuring distances. Hence the sizes of objects are now spoken of in terms of millimetres, centimetres and metres, whereas distances are still measured in yards and miles, rather than metres and kilometres. This is possibly because of the practicality of replacing every signpost in the country. In the 1950s there was no such confusion over the use of two systems. Everything was imperial. All that needed to be known on a daily basis was …

12 inches = 1 foot
3 feet = 1 yard
1,760 yards = 1 mile

But lurking in the past there were some very odd ancillary measurements that schoolchildren, at least at the start of the decade, were required to learn …

22 yards = 1 chain
10 chains = 1 furlong
8 furlongs = 1 mile

Even further back and almost forgotten by then was the fact that there were a little under 8 inches to a link and 100 links to a chain, while rod, pole and perch were three names for the same measurement of 5½ half yards.

Just how these odd measurements came about goes back to 1834, when a government decision to dispose of two cartloads of tally sticks, part of an ancient accounting system no longer in use, led to the unwise decision to burn them in stoves situated in a basement under the House of Lords. As a result, in the early evening of 16 October that year, fire erupted and ignited panelling in the House of Lords before spreading through the House of Commons and, with the exception of a few buildings, decimating the Palace

Signposts in the 1950s had distances designated in miles and fractions of miles, and the tradition still remains.

MAKING CONVERSIONS

There are no direct conversion tables from the old imperial measurements to today's decimal and metric measurements, since the two systems do not compare like with like. In weights and measures, 1 pound was equivalent to 453.6 grams or a little under half a kilo; an inch measured 2.54 centimetres and a yard was the equivalent of 91.44cm – or, to put it another way, there were 39.37 inches in a metre.

For money, one shilling was the equivalent of five decimal pence, and since there were twelve predecimal pennies to a shilling, an old money penny was worth a little less than half a decimal penny. To evaluate how costs of the 1950s compare with today, it is useful to know that £1 in 1950 was equivalent to about £36 today.

Temperatures in the 1950s were usually quoted on the Fahrenheit scale. To convert a temperature in Fahrenheit to today's Centigrade or Celsius scale, it is necessary to deduct 32 from the figure, then divide by 9 and multiply by 5.

of Westminster. Among the many valuable items lost in the fire were the standards of the imperial units of measurement. It meant that there was no longer a criterion by which to confirm the actual dimensions of inches, feet and yards, as well as some of the more obscure units of measurement in use at the time.

To rectify that, astronomer and mathematician George Airy was tasked with creating new standard units of measurement. It took him four years and, to ensure that the measurements were never lost again, they were set in brass, triplicated and, in 1876, embedded in three London landmarks. One set of measurements is to be found in the Great Hall of

The units of measurements devised by mathematician George Airy and embedded into steps in London's Trafalgar Square.

the Guildhall; the second beside the gates of the Royal Observatory in Greenwich; and the third in steps on the north side of Trafalgar Square, leading up to the National Gallery. They can still be seen there today.

When it came to counting money, weighing objects, measuring temperatures, sizes and distances, the necessity to learn some very odd combinations of numbers and, indeed, the names of all the units involved, was not easy. It was, however, something that everyone in the 1950s accepted as part of everyday life.

Chapter 3

The Happiest Days of Your Life

Infant, junior and secondary schools – corporal and physical punishment in the classroom – free milk and healthcare – school dinners

---

FACT BOX

- Children faced a full day's schooling from the age of 5 onwards.
- The baby boom generation led to large class numbers in the 1950s.
- Children were allowed to leave school at 15 throughout the decade.
- Radio programmes played a role in daily lessons.
- Most pupils learned to play the recorder as part of their classwork.
- Punishment by a cane across the hand or buttocks was common in schools.
- Most pupils agreed that school dinners were disgusting.

Schoolchildren of the 1950s would have been clear on their thoughts about whoever it was who coined the epithet about schooldays being the happiest days of their lives. The culprit, they knew, was two things: an adult, and one with a bad memory. Later, they might have agreed that, compared to the trials and tribulations of adulthood, schooldays probably were happier. But it didn't seem like it at the time.

There were no preschool nurseries to ease children into the prospect of what life would be like at school. Quite simply, one day when a child was 5 years old, or as early as 4½ if their birthday fell at a certain time of year, their mother or father – and it was usually their mother, since their father was at work – took them to this building at 9 am in the morning and left them there in charge of a complete stranger in a room full of other, unfamiliar children. Because schools for the very young were usually close to most people's homes, and because mothers rarely worked, there was a good chance that the child would be met at lunchtime and taken home for a meal, before being returned at 2 pm and left there again until

Teacher and pupils from a typical junior school class of the 1950s. The same teacher would have been likely to have taught the same class for four years.

4 pm. It was not at all unusual for some children to be led from the house in tears each morning at the prospect of spending yet another whole day at school.

All of which makes schools of the 1950s sound positively Dickensian. In fact, they weren't. True, they were places of learning, and the learning began from day one, but equally there was time, in the early days of school at least, for activities like painting and drawing or model making, there were playtimes in the playground mid-morning and mid-afternoon, and there was storytelling when the teacher would read to the class sitting cross-legged on the floor. It was rarely too long before even the most recalcitrant child accepted that life had changed and to go, if not always happily but at least with calm acceptance, to school from 9 am to 4 pm five days a week.

Many of the school buildings dated back to Victorian times. A typical design from that era comprised a ground floor where the infants attended, a first floor for juniors and a top floor for seniors, although by the 1950s the senior schools had been mostly replaced by separate secondary schools in different locations. The school building was surrounded by playgrounds, usually separated by age groups. Inside, the design was a large hall, perhaps with a small stage at one end, with doors to classrooms leading off three sides, the fourth containing windows. Toilets, separated for girls and boys, were usually in the playgrounds. Large iron radiators

Schools like this one in Bedfordshire were built in the Victorian era, but were still being extensively used in the 1950s, and continue to be used today.

heated the classrooms, but they were equally likely to have had fireplaces where coal fires could be lit, or oil stoves for cold winter days.

Schools of the time were inevitably overcrowded with as many as fifty in a class. This was largely down to the post-war baby boom. Men returning from the Second World War, which ended in 1945, had often been separated from loved ones for many years, and top of the list when husbands and wives were reunited was to start a family. A great many children of what became known as the Baby Boom Generation were 5 years old and ready for school by 1950 or 1951. Hence the large class sizes, a factor that would follow this generation right through their school years.

The fathers of children at school in the 1950s might have left school at 14, but the Education Act of 1944 had raised the leaving age to 15. So pupils who began school at the age of 5 had at least ten years of education ahead of them. It was more common, however, to stay at school until the age of 16, but it would be 1972 before 16 became the compulsory leaving age. In most parts of the country, the education system was divided into three periods, defined by age.

The three ages of education

From the age of 5 to 7, children attended infant school. Here, they mixed pleasurable pursuits like art with basic learning summed up by the immensely inaccurately named Three Rs: reading, writing and arithmetic (pronounced 'reading, riting and rithmetic'). In the very early years of the decade it wasn't unusual for children to be issued with a slate and a piece of chalk rather than paper and pencil. Likewise, teachers illustrated their words by chalking on a blackboard, a system that continued right through the decade and beyond. To learn how to read and write, children discovered the sounds that different letters made and were taught how to apply those sounds phonetically to words. Arithmetic – a term used then for basic mathematics – gave them the rudimentary aspects of addition, subtraction, multiplication and division. The coronation of Queen Elizabeth II in June 1953 had a tremendous cultural impact on early learning, with children understanding a little about what the monarchy represented, while being encouraged to paint and draw their idea of the event or collect coronation souvenirs and, for those close enough to the capital, with coach trips to London to see the coronation decorations. By the time children of the 1950s left their infant schools, they had the basic knowledge of the Three Rs – and had learned how to correctly spell two of them.

From 7 to 11, children went on to junior school. Previously they might have sat on child-size chairs at low tables, but now they had real desks. A popular style was twin desks joined together with lift-up lids where books were kept and a hard wooden bench seat that each pupil shared with one other. Every desk contained an inkwell and writing was carried out using pens with nibs that had to be regularly dipped in the ink. The common practice was to seat a boy and a girl together on each of the bench seats.

There was still time here for cultural pursuits like art, and it was the place where many learned to play the recorder, but mostly junior school was about learning. By now it was expected that a child could read 'proper' books, as opposed to those designed for elementary reading. Among these, however, there were books aimed specifically at children: Enid Blyton's prestigious range of books for children of all ages from *Noddy and Big Ears* to the *Famous Five* and *Secret Seven* were especially popular for outside school leisure reading, although they wouldn't be seen

Learning to play the recorder was part of junior school lessons for many.

inside the classroom. Children entering junior school were also expected to be capable of writing simple stories, but their writing progressed from capital and small letters to joined-up writing. (The term 'lower case', which actually harks back to the world of printing, wasn't coined for what were then referred to as 'small letters' until the computer age.) On the arithmetic side, they learned their times tables starting at the two times table and finishing with the twelve times table, all memorised by repetition, as classes of children sat reciting, 'one times six is six, two times six is twelve, three times six is eighteen ...' all the way up to 'twelve times six is seventy-two'. Arithmetic also began to cover the mysteries – and, for some, the agonies – of long multiplication and long division. Other subjects covered included English language, geography, history, some basic science, physical education and music. Junior school traversed four years and it wasn't unusual for every year to be in the same classroom with the same teacher covering all the subjects every day of the four years.

At the end of the fourth year came the dreaded Eleven-Plus examination that had been introduced in 1944, replacing the older scholarships, to determine what kind of school each pupil would go on to. The types of secondary school differed around the UK, but by and large they could be divided into three types: grammar schools for the academically minded, technical schools for those whose abilities were more technical than academic, and secondary modern schools for everyone else. As well as writing, arithmetic and spelling to evaluate academic ability, the Eleven-Plus also tested children's powers of reasoning, with problem-solving questions similar to simple IQ tests. If a pupil passed the Eleven-Plus he or she went to a grammar or technical school. Those who failed went to a secondary modern. If a pupil attained a mark right on the borderline of pass and fail, there might be the opportunity to take a resit. Those who also came borderline in that had a final chance of an oral examination, like a one-to-one interview with the headmaster or headmistress, at a specific school.

So, from 11 to 16, children attended one of their chosen secondary schools. Until then, schools were probably mixed, but now it was more likely that they would be segregated into separate establishments for boys and girls. Education was paramount. There was still time in the curriculum for physical education, games, art and music, but the emphasis was now heavily on learning. As arithmetic turned into mathematics, lessons in the way numbers could be juggled into theorems, the understanding of geometry, trigonometry, sines, cosines, tangents and logarithms fascinated some and baffled many. The basics of English language learning became more complicated by the worlds of clause analysis and complicated tenses. English literature, which until then had involved only the enjoyment of reading books that appealed to young

Beal High School at Ilford, Essex, as it is today. The buildings at the back of the main entrance were originally part of Beal Grammar School for Boys, which opened in 1957.

minds, turned into something more boring as pupils were forced to read the classics and endeavour to understand Shakespeare. Chemistry, physics, history and geography were also to the fore, and one period a week was given over to Religious Instruction (RI), strictly confined to Christianity. Later, the lessons would be known as Religious Education (RE) and then Religious Knowledge (RK). Woodwork and metalwork were also taught. While children at technical schools picked up skills in basic engineering and technical drawing, grammar schools taught languages, nearly always French, occasionally German and, for the most academically minded, Latin. Meanwhile, the secondary modern schools took on similar subjects, though rarely languages, all aimed at pupils with slightly less leaning ability. It didn't make them less important than technical or grammar schools and many pupils who ended up doing badly at a grammar school might have benefited more from an education better suited to their abilities at a secondary modern.

At 16, those that hadn't left school at 15 took their O-Level GCE (O for ordinary, GCE for General Certificate of Education) examinations, with separate papers for each of the subjects they had been studying for the past five years, but with particular emphasis on the curriculum of the past year or so. GCE exams were introduced in 1951. Those deemed

Most secondary schools were equipped with science labs whose desks contained sinks, as well as multiple gas points for the attachment of Bunsen burners.

good enough to go on could then take a further two years of education in a few specialised subjects for which they took their A-Level GCEs (A for advanced) up until the age of 18. According to those results, there was a slim opportunity to go on to higher education at a university. That was the theory, anyway. The fact is that in the 1950s and even into the 1960s, few who took O-Levels went on to A-Levels and only an extremely small selection of A-Level students were ever selected for university. This selection was made worse by the fact that, apart from a few universities that were rather looked down upon, none would take even a top performing A-Level student if he or she hadn't previously passed O-Level Latin.

So, at the end of a 1950s school pupil's life, a few left for work at the age of 15, most left school at 16, a small selection went on to leave at 18, and an even smaller selection of those made it to university. And in all these years, the main means of communication between teacher and pupils was by way of chalk on a blackboard.

School punishments

In the modern age when teachers only have to touch a pupil to risk charges of molestation, it's difficult to imagine the ease and frequency with which teachers of the 1950s were entitled to slap, poke, beat and generally strike children with implements that ranged from rulers and canes to well-aimed pieces of chalk.

One extremely boring, laborious, though non-violent, means of punishment consisted of forcing pupils to 'write lines'. This involved sitting down with a pen and a piece of paper on which was written the same sentence over and over again for as many times as requested by the teacher, usually 100 times. If the given sentence was as simple as 'I must not talk', the common method was to write 'I, I, I, I ...' down one side of the paper, then add 'must, must, must, must ...' beside it followed by the rest of the sentence, one word, one line at a time. Many teachers, however, took it into their heads to make the required sentence, or line, as complicated as possible; 'Making excessive noise during a lesson is to be avoided at all times' was the kind of thing that depressed all those who were forced to stay behind after school to complete their hundred or more lines.

In an infant school, the main punishment for a misbehaving child would be a stern talking to and an invitation to spend the rest of the lesson standing in a corner. But when a pupil made the transition from infant to junior school, corporal punishment entered his or her life. A particularly naughty boy might be pulled out in front of the class and the teacher, who, only a few minutes before had been benignly explaining the difference between the words 'to', 'too' and 'two', suddenly turned into a sadist who held a boy's wrist in one hand while bringing down a cane sharply on his outstretched palm.

A cartoon from 1888 shows pupils receiving the cane, a practice that was still prevalent in the 1950s.

Little girls were not subjected to the cane in this way but were likely to have a ruler administered to the backs of their legs.

The next move to secondary school saw corporal punishment take a turn for the worse, as vicious teachers administered the cane, sometimes as many as six strokes at a time across the buttocks, and inappropriately known as 'six of the best'. Those who received the punishments were rarely allowed to explain themselves or to appeal against the judgement. Most schools operated a regime of cane first, ask questions later. Many received the cane unjustly because a teacher mistook the pupil for a wrong-doer, while the real culprits managed to make a getaway. Some teachers really were sadistic. It was not unusual for one to slap a pupil heavily around the head if, as he passed a desk, he suspected someone was talking when they shouldn't. Others were known for the accuracy with which they could hurl a piece of chalk or even a heavy blackboard chalk rubber across the room at someone suspected of misbehaving. Poking in the chest with a hard finger was also a way that some teachers had of instilling important facts into a pupil's head.

All of these either planned or sometimes just spontaneous outbreaks of teacher violence were allowed without parental consent, and it was rare for a parent to complain even if their child had been punished unjustly. It was very much accepted that corporal punishment in general and caning in particular was all part of school life, necessary to retain discipline. Corporal punishment was finally outlawed in British schools in 1986.

School milk

Following the post-war general election in 1945, Member of Parliament Ellen Wilkinson was appointed as Minister of Education. A long campaigner against poverty, she was responsible for the School Milk Act of 1946, which made it law that every schoolboy or girl under the age of 18 should be given a free ⅓-pint bottle of milk every school day. Not all school pupils of the 1950s would have thanked her for her efforts.

The milk was handed out mid-morning and many thought it hideous. The main problem was that the milk was delivered in crates each morning

One-third of a pint of milk, taken at desks, was an everyday occurrence at schools in the 1950s.

and, by the time it reached the desks of pupils who sat, straws at the ready, to drink it, the milk was past its best. If it was a nice cool day, it wasn't so bad. But if it was a hot summer's day, then the milk was tepid and tasteless. Even worse, if the day was really cold, the milk was likely to have frozen while standing in the playground waiting to be brought into classrooms. It would then have to be defrosted by warming it up in front of radiators. The result was another ⅓-pint of warm, tasteless liquid. Sometimes there might be two or three bottles over after they had all been given out. These would be put on a windowsill and later that day, usually around mid-afternoon, a bottle might be awarded to a pupil as a special prize for excelling in a piece of work. By that time, warmed by the sun through the window, or a radiator below, the milk was watery and the layer of thick cream on the top had curdled.

In 1968, the Labour government cut free milk to secondary schools, where few pupils bothered to drink it anyway. In 1971, Conservative Prime Minister Edward Heath gave instructions to Margaret Thatcher, at that time Secretary of State for Education, to cut free milk for children over 7. Despite the fact that the command had come from above and Mrs Thatcher was in fact against the idea, she became labelled 'Thatcher the Milk Snatcher'. It was a slur that she carried with her right through to the days when she served as Prime Minister

Singing, dancing and physical training

In infant and junior schools, the school hall was the venue for many non-academic lessons, and it was a place where radios and gramophones played a big part.

In 1947, the School Broadcasting Council for the United Kingdom had been set up to provide educational and musical programmes to supplement lessons for schoolchildren. Prime among these was a programme called *Music and Movement*. At a specific time of day and day of the week when the programme was due to be broadcast, children were ushered out of the classroom and into the hall. Most schools had a large radio secreted away somewhere with extension loudspeakers in the hall and in the classrooms. With the radio turned on and tuned in to the morning's schools broadcast, children found themselves being told to pretend they were all sorts of things like frogs, snakes or even daffodils and to do it to music. The radio announcer could be heard saying things like, 'Now, children we are all going to be trees. Raise your arms and pretend they are branches. Now let's all sway in the wind.' Little girls thought it was fun. Little boys thought it was silly and embarrassing. For many a shy child it was one of the most excruciating times of the week.

Back in the classroom, another radio programme called *Singing Together* encouraged children to sit at their desks and sing songs that usually took the form of old folk songs and sea shanties like 'Soldier, Soldier, Won't You Marry Me?' and 'The Raggle-Taggle Gypsies'. It wasn't quite as embarrassing as *Music and Movement*, but it was close.

Maximum embarrassment, especially for boys, however, occurred with the weekly trip back into the hall for a session of country dancing. Accompanied by scratchy old seventy-eight revolutions per minute 10-inch records on the school gramophone, classes were taught the intricacies of traditional dances like 'Dashing White Sergeant', 'Pat-a-cake Polka' and the 'Cumberland Square Eight'. The dances were designed for boys and girls to dance together, but inevitably the girls wanted nothing to do with touching smelly boys and paired off to dance alone, leaving thoroughly embarrassed groups of boys to dance with each other.

Physical exercise, which also took place in the hall, came with regular PT lessons. PT stood for Physical Training, which later was amended to PE for Physical Education. No one had PT kits. The lesson was taken with boys stripping down to vests and underpants, girls in their vests and knickers, and everyone in bare feet, as the class went through a set series of exercises.

All of this was left behind when pupils graduated to secondary schools, where there were no more music-based exercise activities. Many secondary schools had their own gymnasiums where more formalised physical training and sports were undertaken while wearing purpose-made shorts, shirts and plimsolls.

Staying healthy

In infant and junior schools of the 1950s, there was an obsession with making sure children stayed healthy. There were visits from the school dentist and optician to check pupils' teeth and eyesight, and what was universally known as the nit nurse was also a regular visitor. For her visits,

Schoolchildren
line up for dental
examinations.

Children line up for their vaccinations.

SCHOOL PHOTOGRAPHS

Photographers were intermittent visitors to schools in the 1950s. Conventionally they set up portable studios to take pictures of each pupil individually, for selling on to parents and other doting relatives. Occasionally, however, a school would be visited by a very special photographer who took one exposure of the entire school and delivered it as a super-wide picture rolled up in a cardboard tube. These were taken by a camera called a Cirkut which, despite dating back to as early as 1900, continued to be used in schools throughout the

A Cirkut camera, the type that took super-wide panoramic pictures of school pupils.

1950s and for many years after. These panoramic picture photographers usually attended secondary, rather than infant or junior, schools.

The photographer's visit would have started long before the appointed time for the picture to be taken. He and his assistant would arrive in the playground and

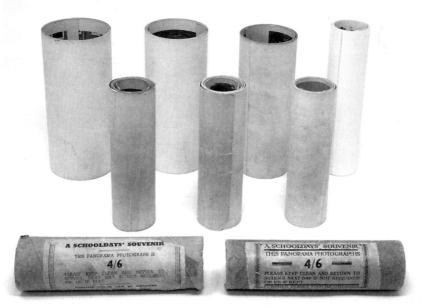

The panoramic pictures were sent back to parents rolled in cardboard tubes. In the 1950s they cost 4s 6d per picture.

produce a long rope with a huge weight on one end and a big chunk of chalk on the other. The photographer chalked a cross on the playground, then placed the weighted end of the rope on the centre of the cross. While his assistant stood on this to keep it in position the photographer used the tightly drawn rope to inscribe an enormous chalk arc on the ground. Next, various pieces of furniture were moved out into the playground: mats and benches from the gym, chairs from classrooms and tables from the dining hall, all to be arranged around the chalked arc.

Later, the entire school trooped outside for the photograph. The smallest children sat cross-legged on the mats with slightly taller pupils kneeling behind them. Behind that row more pupils and teachers sat on chairs, and behind them another row stood. Behind that row, older pupils sat on chairs arranged on the tables and the last row stood on the tables behind the chairs.

The camera, set up in front of this arc, was huge and balanced on the top of a tall wooden tripod with the camera lens pointing to one side of the group. The photographer inserted a key and wound it up. Someone blew a whistle, which was everyone's cue to look straight ahead and on no account move their heads. The photographer pressed a lever and, to the astonishment of all, the camera began to revolve on its tripod, driven by a whirring clockwork motor as it swept across the huge arc of children from one side to the other. During this movement, film was also moving inside the camera, across the body and past a slit behind the lens. In this way, a super-wide image was built up on the film.

The joke when these pictures were taken was that, as the camera began to revolve, someone standing on the extreme left of the group could run very fast behind the line-up to take their place on the extreme right before the camera reached that spot. Hence the same person would appear twice in the photograph. It was a good idea in theory and many a schoolboy (not many schoolgirls) tried it, though it rarely worked out in practice. The boy soon discovered that the

An entire school captured on one super-wide panoramic picture in 1957.

distance behind a semi-circular arc was further than expected and, even running at full speed, risking the possibility of tripping and negating the whole thing, it was difficult to get to the other end before the camera completed its circuit. What was more, if he took off too early his presence at the spot where he should have been seen was either empty or discernible only as an indefinable blur. In the end, rather than appearing twice in the picture, there was a good chance that he didn't appear at all. And, once found out, he was likely to have got the cane for his troubles.

everyone lined up, each to be examined in turn as the nurse combed through hair to check for head lice and to make sure there was no infestation.

In the early 1950s, a worldwide epidemic broke out of a disease called poliomyelitis, better known simply as polio. It could be spread by droplets in the air and resulted in flu-like symptoms that included sore throat, fever, tiredness, nausea, headache and stomach pains. In some sufferers it could also lead to an attack on the nervous system, resulting in numbness, and in the worst cases, severe paralysis. In the early 1950s, a vaccine was developed in America and by 1956 it was being administered to all British schoolchildren, who received it on a sugar lump.

There were no vaccinations against diseases like measles, mumps and whooping cough, and in fact most children contracted each or any of these nasty illnesses before they were 7 or 8 years old. Once recovered they were immune for the rest of their lives.

At secondary school level, pupils were vaccinated against tuberculosis, with the BCG – standing for Bacillus Calmette-Guérin – vaccination, this time with a more traditional needle at the top of the arm.

School dinners

Strictly speaking, the meals served up to schoolchildren who didn't go home midway through the day were lunches. But they were known universally as school dinners and, by and large, they were awful. The cost for most of the decade was a shilling a day, collected by teachers each morning after the register had been called to ascertain who was present or absent. There were several reasons why the dinners were so bad, one of which was post-war austerity, which meant so much was on ration, with meat being the last to go. Another reason was that the dinners were not always cooked on the school premises. At infant and junior schools in particular, they were cooked in central council-run kitchens somewhere in the town and then transported in huge metal containers to schools throughout the area. Inevitably, everything was cold or, at best, lukewarm by the time it got to tables. Later, at secondary school, it was more likely that a school would have its own kitchen where dinner ladies came to cook every day.

Dinner is served, as children of the 1950s line up to receive the first course.

Mince making in a school kitchen, with a bucket of cabbage at the ready.

While meat was still on ration, mince was part of the daily diet. Greasy and full of gristle, it would be accompanied by a couple of vegetables, usually mashed potato and over-boiled green cabbage. When meat came off ration and became more freely available it wasn't much better because, along with the mashed potato and cabbage regulars, came a piece of meat that was small, square, extremely tough and with origins that were unidentifiable. Chips belonged to a different world and were rarely, if ever, to be seen on a school dinner plate.

The second course, commonly known as 'afters', was always something and custard. The 'something' was sometimes some kind of bland suet pudding. Occasionally, if the young diners had been lucky enough to find a piece of Yorkshire pudding on their plates as part of the first course, what was left over was served up again with custard for 'afters', with grease from the batter oozing into the custard. Because classes were large, there were often two sittings for dinner, which meant everyone was forced to eat very fast.

Even those who eventually conceded that schooldays were happier than expected would have been loath to extend their memories of happiness to the half hour or so of frantic fast eating of rubbish food that encapsulated school dinners of the 1950s.

Chapter 4

Toys for the Boys (and Girls)

*Meccano – model railways – Dinky Toys – Corgi cars –
Mr Potato Head – building sets – Barbie and Sindy*

FACT BOX

- Inventor Frank Hornby was responsible for three of the most popular boys' toys: Meccano, Hornby railways and Dinky Toys.
- Tri-ang rivalled both Hornby railways and Dinky Toys.
- Most toy advertisements were aimed at boys.
- Barbie began life as a risqué German comic strip and a doll aimed at adults.
- Mr Potato Head began life in the 1950s but today, for reasons of political correctness, has had 'Mr' removed from his name.
- Silly putty was invented by accident.

It's unlikely that many children at the start of the 1950s, or even some years into the decade, were playing with new toys. Many would have been second-hand, or left over from a previous generation. Those that

Peddle cars and bikes were favourite toys of the 1950s.

were purchased new would rarely have been newly designed. Many of the toys still very popular in the 1950s were first patented and manufactured many years before. That said, it wasn't too long into the decade before some of those earlier toys, whose potential improvements had been interrupted by the Second World War, were resurrected and updated to win the hearts of many a child. Of all the toys that went through this process, the name of one company and one man stands out as the creator of three major names destined to go down in history as classics. The company was Meccano Ltd which, during the 1920s and 1930s, was the biggest toy manufacturer in Britain. The man behind it was inventor, businessman and politician Frank Hornby.

Meccano

Frank Hornby was born in 1863 and married in 1887. He had two sons and a daughter. Despite having no formal training as an engineer, he began making model cranes for his sons, using perforated metal strips held together with small nuts and bolts. The important feature was the way the nuts and bolts in the finished model could be undone in order to dismantle the model and so use the metal strips to build something else. Seeing the potential for turning the idea into a commercially sold toy, Hornby set out to mass produce the components, for which he was granted a patent in 1901.

The toy was first sold under the name Mechanics Made Easy, but that was changed to Meccano in 1907, and the company name Meccano Limited was registered in 1908. In the years ahead, production increased fast. In 1914, a factory was opened in Liverpool to manufacture the Meccano parts, and soon there were factories at Speke and Aintree too, as well as manufacturing bases in Argentina, France, Germany, America and Spain. In 1916, the company published the monthly *Meccano Magazine*, which was still going strong in the 1950s.

Frank Hornby died in 1936, but his legacy lived on and, by the 1950s, Meccano was one of the most popular toys among engineering-minded children. It was sold in kits, numbered from 0 to 10, and every kit contained more and differently shaped parts than the previous one. Each kit number could be converted to the next one up with an upgrade kit. The main components of any Meccano set were plates of different sizes

Meccano magazines from 1950, 1951 and 1952.

Meccano advertisement from July 1950.

Meccano gears outfits added more versatility to building projects.

and shapes with girders and metal strips of various lengths. These were all perforated with holes at uniform distances, to enable them to be bolted together in any desired configuration. The kits also contained spindles of different lengths and wheels of varying diameters, some equipped with metal or rubber tyres, others with grooves to be used as pulleys.

Coloured parts replaced the natural metal colours in 1926 to mark the twenty-fifth anniversary of Hornby's patent. Light red was used for the plates, pea green for the metal strips, silver for spindles and black for wheels. A year later, the red and green colours of the components were darkened. In the 1930s, the kits changed colours to blue for the plates and gold for the strips, but only in the UK. Exported kits were still red and green, colours that were reinstated in Britain following the end of the Second World War. So, by the 1950s, all the kits were red and green again. The number 10 set was the most prestigious and sought after by junior engineers, as well as the most expensive prospect for their parents. Later, accessory sets of gear wheels were introduced. Motors were also available, first driven by clockwork and later battery driven.

Meccano remained immensely popular throughout the 1950s, but by the early 1960s, Meccano Ltd was having financial problems. The company was taken over in 1964 by Lines Brothers Limited, who traded as Tri-ang. This was the first of a great many takeovers and acquisitions that followed in the years ahead, as its component colours were changed yet again. But it's the old red and green sets of the 1950s that remain in the hearts and minds of so many boys, who went on to pursue careers in engineering thanks to Meccano, and it was the 1950s that probably saw the major peak in the toy's popularity.

Hornby trains

After the First World War, when consumers were loath to buy German products, Frank Hornby began making clockwork trains, first as construction kits, later ready assembled. They were made in the '0' gauge, which was defined as 1:48, or one quarter of an inch to the foot. Originally, the trains ran by clockwork, and many of these train sets survived through the Second World War, eventually falling into the hands of children of the 1950s. Layouts were rarely imaginative and little more than a single track that ran around in a circle or a larger

Boys of the early 1950s
were devoted to their
Hornby clockwork
railways.

Clockwork '0' gauge locomotives from Hornby.

oblong with a few accessories like tunnels, stations and signals along the way.

Hornby went on to produce electric versions of his clockwork trains. Early examples ran by mains electricity and were considered unsafe for children. Later, 12-volt systems were introduced, whose low current made it safe for children to touch the electrified rails. Few of these would have been found in the homes of the 1950s. There was, however, one place where children of that era could see a working '0' gauge electric railway in action. Gamages, a large London department store that traded from 1878 until 1972, during the 1950s displayed a huge electric '0' gauge railway for children to see on their way to meeting Father Christmas and his friend Uncle Holly.

After the death of Frank Hornby in 1936, the company continued under the chairmanship of his son Roland. In 1938, the company introduced a new series of electric railway sets in the '00' gauge which strangely mixed imperial with metric measurements to be defined as 4mm to the foot, or 1:76. It became known as Dublo, derived from the phonetic pronunciation of '00' or 'Double 0'.

Production of Hornby Dublo trains was suspended during the Second World War, but resumed shortly after with new locomotives and rolling

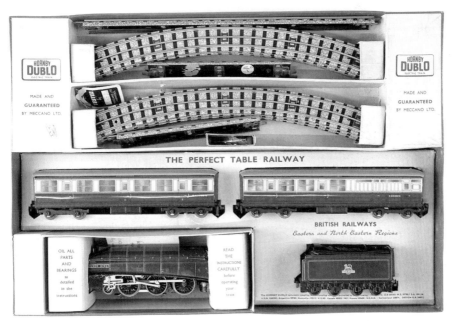

An early Hornby Dublo electric train set with the original three-rail track.

Two Hornby electric locomotives made for the Dublo system.

An advertisement in December 1951 warns Hornby railway enthusiasts that spare parts are becoming hard to come by.

stock introduced at regular intervals throughout the 1950s. With the nationalisation of the railways in 1953, Hornby switched to trains in the liveries of British Railways, which had been formed in 1948.

Depending on how rich they – or their parents – were, children of the 1950s could use the Dublo system to build ambitious layouts that far exceeded the old round-and-round tracks of the past, with trains running on several tracks at the same time, points systems for sidings, crossovers between tracks and more. The size of a model railway layout and its complexity was governed only by the space available for a layout and, of course, the cost of buying all its components.

The '00' gauge was also used by other model railway manufacturers, most notably in Britain by Tri-ang, leading to intense rivalry during the 1950s between those who bought (or more likely had bought for them) either Hornby or Tri-ang trains. Electric railway enthusiasts supported one or the other, but never both. It was a hobby that far transcended the term toy as many children continued building ever better railway layouts into their teens and adulthood. For some, what started as a children's toy in the 1950s turned into a lifelong obsession.

Dinky Toys

The third big toy to emerge from Frank Hornby's Meccano company was the extremely successful and ultimately enormous range of vehicles first sold in 1933 under the name Modelled Miniatures. They were made from die-cast zinc alloy and in 1934 they were renamed Dinky Toys. When they first appeared on the market they were planned as lineside accessories for Hornby railways before becoming popular in their own right. Although simultaneously produced in France, they were made in Britain at the Meccano factory in Liverpool and sold well until the outbreak of war in 1939, when production was suspended. Some pre-war stock made it to the market in 1945, the year the war ended, but proper production didn't begin again until 1946. Even then, many of the toys were re-issues of pre-war vehicles. In 1947, the first Dinky Supertoys were introduced, models of larger vehicles and with more realistic treaded tyres.

So by the start of the 1950s, as production of new models began in earnest, Dinky Toys were well established and much sought after by children who were offered every type of vehicle, including saloon cars,

A 1950s advertisement for Dinky Toys and Supertoys.

sports cars, racing cars, commercial vehicles, military vehicles, even aircraft and ships. Buyers tended to fall into two groups: the users and the collectors. Users discarded any packaging in which the toys arrived and set to playing with them on the rough surfaces of school playgrounds or in the streets, where so many children played in the 1950s. Because Dinky Toys were strictly push-along models without any motors, they were often used in races, or pushed downhill at speeds that inevitably

Dinky Toys that have stood the test of time beyond the 1950s. Left to right: Hudson-Hornet, Ford Devette, Nash Rambler, Hudson Sedan and Rover 75.

Dinky Toys and Supertoys that have been kept in their boxes, like this display of fire engines, are much sought after by today's collectors.

led to them turning over and getting damaged. The collectors thought such behaviour atrocious. Because many Dinky Toys were sold as part of a series, they appealed to children with a collector's instinct for putting together complete sets. Some of the saloon cars, for example, were sold in different colours. The miniature racing cars covered all the colours and the shapes of well-known names in the era's motor racing world. If there were variations on any of the vehicles, collectors needed the complete set, which they invariably kept in their original boxes.

As a result, two types of Dinky Toy have survived today: highly collectable and valuable pristine toys still in their original boxes, and less sought-after seriously scuffed, scratched and scraped examples whose boxes disappeared not long after the toys were bought all those years ago.

Railway rivals

Frank Hornby and his successors who ran Meccano Ltd dominated a major sector of the toy market at the start of the 1950s. But as the decade wore on, and other companies began to get their acts together following the Second World War, new toy manufacturers emerged to challenge Hornby/Meccano's market domination. There were those who attempted to copy the Meccano building sets with similar, but not quite the same,

A Trix Twin model railway outfit that rivalled both Hornby and Tri-ang.

components. But it was clear that Meccano had too solid a grip on that market for rivals to make any real dent in their sales. Model railways, however, were a different matter.

Bassett-Lowke was a well-established, though less well-known, name in model railways, having built models in various gauges long before even the First World War. The company produced its first '00' gauge railways in 1920, and many of these survived into the 1950s, the company going into decline towards the end of the decade. The Trix company produced Trix Twin '00' scale model railways during the 1950s. German Märklin model railways also found their way into a few homes, probably by way of fathers who had brought the toys home from the war. There were also those who bought track from independent makers and built their own engines and rolling stock, either from scratch or from model kits.

The biggest rival to Hornby, and the name that won the hearts and minds of a great many model railway enthusiasts, was Tri-ang. The rivalry that the coming of Tri-ang caused was not only between the manufacturers, it stretched to the users too. Tri-ang enthusiasts made fun of the fact that Hornby railways initially ran on unrealistic three rails, whereas Tri-ang trains ran on the more conventional two rails from the start. Hornby users claimed that their trains were more sophisticated with superior locomotives and better control units. Tri-ang enthusiasts pointed out the early Hornby trains had carriages made of tin plate with windows and the people inside painted on, whereas Tri-ang carriages were made of injection-moulded plastic with real windows … and so it went on.

A kit-built '0' gauge locomotive in London North Eastern Railway (LNER) green livery.

The arrival of Tri-ang

Tri-ang's entry into the market began in 1946, when a small manufacturing company called Rovex Plastics Ltd set up in business in Surrey. They began by making plastic model cars but soon ran into trouble when the Rover car company objected to the use of the name Rovex on the models. Rather than rebrand their goods, the company turned from making model cars to making model railways, with a contract for selling them through the Marks & Spencer chain of stores. The company's first model railways appeared in 1950, but soon after the company ran into financial difficulties. At which point, Lines Brothers Ltd entered the scene.

The Lines Brothers were William, Walter and Arthur Lines, who opened for business in 1919. Before long they had become famous for the manufacture of twenty-seven different styles of doll's house along with miniature doll's furniture, doll's prams, pogo sticks, rocking and push horses, pedal cars, scooters, children's tricycles, model cars, children's desks, furniture for young people, swings, clockwork mechanical toys, model aeroplanes … and more. The Lines Brothers company acquired Rovex in 1951, as a way of getting into the model railway market, which they sold under the Tri-ang name, based on a triangular logo whose three sides represented the three brothers. By 1952, the Marks & Spencer

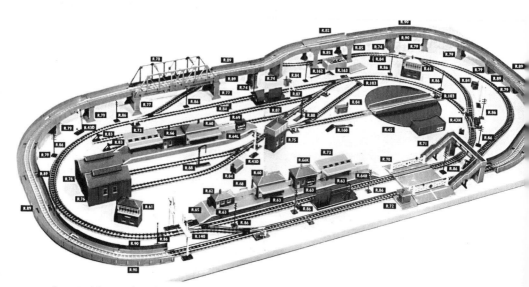

A typical layout that shows the kind of items available from Tri-ang in the mid-1950s. The numbers refer to items listed in that year's Tri-ang railways catalogue.

contract had been cancelled, meaning the model railways were no longer exclusive to the chain store. With the freedom to sell Tri-ang railways to anyone and everyone, the first train sets went on show at the 1952 British Industries Fair. They primarily used the '00' gauge that had been pioneered by Hornby, but also introduced some models in the 'H0' gauge, which involved differently scaled engines and rolling stock that ran on the same tracks.

In 1954, production was shifted from the small Rovex factory in Surrey to a new factory built at Margate in Kent. The first Tri-ang Railways catalogue appeared in 1955 and became an annual delight for model railway enthusiasts over the next decade.

That first catalogue illustrated ten different train sets, eight electric and two clockwork. Each set comprised an engine, carriages, track for a simple oval layout and a control box for use with either built-in batteries or an external transformer that supplied 12 volts from a mains supply. The transformers tended to hum softly and, when hot, gave off a distinctive smell that was for ever associated with electric model railways.

The train sets contained accurate scale replicas of different types of British Railways steam trains and Transcontinental diesel trains. Rolling

Railway items available from Tri-ang in 1959, from that year's catalogue.

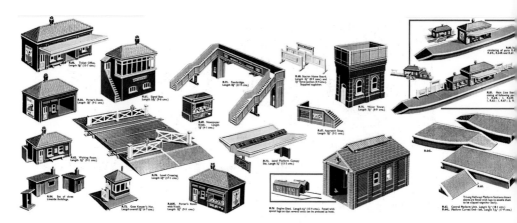

From Tri-ang's 1957 catalogue, some of the accessories available for the company's model railways.

stock included passenger carriages, freight wagons and an operating Royal Mail carriage that automatically picked up a mail bag from one place and delivered it into a box on another part of the track. Accessories included a level crossing, signals, a turntable, model stations, bridges, standard track, points, crossover sections and suggestions for simple layouts. By the end of the decade the 1959 catalogue was showing Tri-ang's new overhead power system, which allowed the engines to pick up their current from either the rails or overhead wires, meaning two engines could be independently run on the same track. By this time a new track had also been introduced which was more realistic compared to the real thing.

In 1965, Hornby and Tri-ang amalgamated. To the delight of Tri-ang enthusiasts, the new company was initially called Tri-ang Hornby. It was later changed to Hornby Railways in 1973, and simply Hornby in 1997. By that time, with the exception of those who continued to be model railway enthusiasts into adulthood and were destined to continue their enthusiasm well into their old age, the majority of children who had once championed either one maker or the other had grown up and moved on to new interests.

Dinky Toy rivals

Tri-ang didn't just rival the Meccano company's Hornby train sets, it also made a range of model cars that rivalled Dinky. They were called Tri-ang

THE BEST OF ALL CHRISTMAS GIFTS

MINIC DUMP TRUCK
Length 4 in.   **Price 3/11**

MINIC LONDON FIRE ENGINE & LADDERS with HOSE
Length 6¼ in.   **Price 9/6 ¾**

MINIC TRACTOR & TRAILER with CASES
Length 7¼ in.   **Price 4/6**
Tractor only.   **Price 2/11**

MINIC MECHANICAL HORSE & LOG TRAILER
Length 7½ in.   **Price 4/11**

MINIC PRESENTATION SET Nº 2

A word in the right quarter and we are sure you'll be the happy owner of these fine MINIC Presentation Sets this Christmas. Its a grand way of starting a MINIC fleet—and collecting MINICS is a very popular hobby these days.

Each set contains a selection of the favourite MINICS—Britain's most famous CLOCKWORK TOYS. MINIC Presentation Set No. 2 contains the Dustcart, Morris Minor, Post Office Telephone Van, Delivery Lorry, Vauxhall Cabriolet, No. 1 Racer, Streamline Sports and Tractor . . . and **26/11** it only costs

Other Sets are priced at 7/11, 10/6, 15/6 and 25/-. All 70 models in the range are, of course, available singly.

Ask to see them at your local toy shop— we do not supply direct.

Tri-ang Toys

REGD. TRADE MARK

Manufactured by
LINES BROS. LTD., MERTON, LONDON S.W.19, ENGLAND

Minic toys available from Tri-ang in 1950.

Spot-On model cars from Tri-ang.

Minics, and they were advertised as scale models of the latest cars, lorries, buses, tractors, armoured cars – in fact, every type of vehicle. An August 1950 Tri-ang advertisement proclaimed that there were seventy different models. By November the following year, advertisements claimed eighty models, and also a Minic service station that included a clockwork-driven lift. The vehicles also featured clockwork motors that gave them a strong advantage over Dinky Toys, which were mainly push-along models. Tri-ang also sold a series of vehicles under the name Spot-On.

Dinky's biggest rival, however, was Corgi, whose model cars were introduced to the UK in 1956. Corgi took a different approach to Dinky. Whereas Dinky Toys were known for their traditional, and maybe a little old-fashioned, approach, Corgi came in with modern, up-to-the-minute vehicles, often tied in with films or TV programmes.

Corgi toys were made in Wales by a company called Mettoy, derived from the words 'metal toys'. Like so many other toys of the 1950s, Corgis had their roots in the past, this time in a factory set up by German-born Phillip Ullmann in 1933. The company began by making tinplate vehicles, moving on after the Second World War to solid, and rather crudely made, solid metal toys, then into die-cast toys that were robustly made but still lacking any real detail. In 1954, the company produced two British cars – a Standard Vanguard and a Rolls Royce, followed by other vehicles. While fairly successful, they were still no match for Dinky Toys.

In the mid-1950s, Mettoy switched production into a range that really went after Dinky. With a new factory based in South Wales, the name Corgi was chosen. It was well suited, being the name of a small but sturdy Welsh dog and also a word similar to, though not the same as, Dinky. Their big claim to fame at the start was the fact that they had real plastic windows and would later go on to even more realistic designs

Corgi toys that have stood the test of time: Jaguar Mark X (in front) and Karrier Bantam.

and innovations that included bonnets that opened to reveal detailed engines, jewelled headlights, working windscreen wipers and real steering mechanisms. The first Corgis, launched at the British Industries Fair in 1956, were a Ford Consul, Austin Cambridge, Morris Cowley, Riley Pathfinder, Vauxhall Velox, Rover 90 and Hillman Husky.

For the rest of the 1950s, Corgi went on to produce more and better toys, until really making a name for themselves in 1965 with the release of an Aston Martin DB5 that tied in with the James Bond film *Goldfinger*. The car in the film had a wealth of gadgets, the most famous of which was an injector seat that catapulted the passenger though the sunroof. The Corgi version did the same. It was released in November 1965, sold more than a million by Christmas and topped 4 million during its four years of production.

Dinky's other big rival was the Matchbox series of vehicles made by Moko Lesney, a British toymaking company formed in 1947. The small die-cast vehicles appeared first in 1953. Unlike their rivals, Matchbox

Matchbox toys came in small boxes only slightly larger than normal matchboxes.

toys made no attempt at producing the series in a unified scale. The only requirement of size was that the toy vehicle should fit into a uniform sized box that was slightly larger than a standard matchbox. Hence, a large double-decker bus was made in a similar physical size, though in a totally different scale, to a small sports car, something that model railway enthusiasts, looking for vehicles to populate the roads around their railway layouts, found very frustrating.

Toys for the girls

Considering everything that has gone before it might be assumed that toys in the 1950s were aimed only at boys, and a glance in any toyshop window of the time would have done little to dispel this idea. By later standards, it was a somewhat chauvinistic age. Boys played with masculine toys like model railways, cars and soldiers as well as building and construction sets that would to some extent guide them into future careers; girls played with dolls, prams and toy versions of household appliances that would guide them into a life of motherhood and housewifery.

Toy advertisements unashamedly aimed themselves at one sex or the other, with little thought of possible crossovers of interests. Girls were not

Give Your Boy
Meccano this Christmas

LET your boy use his hands and brains to build his own Toys. With Meccano any boy can build hundreds of real working models in shining steel— Transporter Bridges, like the one shown here ; Motor Cars that run ; Cranes that will raise real loads ; Looms that will weave real ties and ribbons ; Lathes that will turn.

Meccano building is delightfully simple—endlessly fascinating.   No skill or study needed.   The big Book of Instructions makes everything clear.

Complete Outfits 6/- to 180/-

MECCANO

MECCANO LAND

INTERESTING STORY BOOK **FREE** TO BOYS.

This is a real story of a boy's journey into a sunny land where all is happiness and fun ; where dullness is never known.   A splendid story for boys.

How to get a Free copy.

Just show this page to three chums and send us their names and addresses with your own.   Put No. 43 after your name for reference.

Write To-day.

Meccano Ltd : Binns Road : Liverpool

A Meccano advertisement shows how the toy was aimed at boys, while girls were only allowed to look on in admiration.

supposed to be interested in building things, any more than boys might take the slightest interest in dolls. An early Meccano advertisement sums up the attitude nicely, in which a girl is pictured looking on admiringly while a boy does all the work, building an enormous suspension bridge. The blurb beside the picture doesn't even acknowledge the girl:

> Let your boy use his hands and brains to build his own toys. With Meccano any boy can build hundreds of real working models – transporter bridges, motor cars that run, cranes that will raise real loads, looms that will weave ties and ribbons, lathes that will turn. Meccano building is delightfully simple, endlessly fascinating. No skill or study needed. The big book of instructions makes everything clear.

And then, in 1959, Barbie arrived. Barbie was born in America but soon found her way to Britain on the way to becoming a global icon, selling 300,000 dolls in her first year of production. She was unlike any of the dolls that little girls in Britain had seen before, most of which were styled as babies, or at least small children; Barbie was anything but. She was advertised as a teenage fashion model, but a teenager that was distinctly American, as opposed to British teenagers of the 1950s. Her full name, her buyers were told, was Barbara Millicent Roberts, and she lived in the town of Willows in Wisconsin.

The first model was known as Ponytail Barbie, because of her hairstyle, and she was available as either a blonde or a brunette. Barbie arrived with red lips, black eyeliner, perfectly manicured eyebrows – and a figure that was totally alien to doll designs of the time, shown off in her zebra-striped strapless swimsuit. Other clothes, in distinctive 1950s fashion styles, were available for little girls to buy and dress their Barbies according to their tastes.

Born at the end of the 1950s, the 1960s saw Barbie evolve into many different incarnations and gain friends, including her boyfriend Ken. In 1963, her dominance of the market was challenged by Sindy,

The first Ponytail Barbie in her zebra-striped swimsuit.

BARBIE'S SEXY PAST

No one could deny that Barbie, unlike any doll before her, was actually sexy. So it's not surprising that her inspiration was another doll based on a slightly risqué German comic strip character and initially sold, not to children, but as an adult novelty doll that could be undressed and dressed again in different clothes. Her name was Bild Lilli and she was first sold in Germany in 1955. The following year, American businesswoman Ruth Handler spotted Lilli while on holiday in Switzerland. She bought three dolls, took them home and introduced them to the Mattel toy company, co-founded by her husband Eliot. Together they transformed Lilli into Barbie – and the rest is history.

---

an English rival produced by Pedigree Dolls and Toys, a division of the Lines Brothers toy manufacturing companies. Between them, Barbie and Sindy changed the way little girls thought about playing with dolls – and were quite possibly responsible for not a few little boys also taking an interest for the first time.

Mr Potato Head

Some toys of course were unisex, not that children, or anyone else in the 1950s, would have understood that word, first used in a copy of *Life* magazine in 1968. Board games like Drafts that date back to around 3000 BC and Snakes and Ladders, which can be traced to the second century, were as popular as ever in the 1950s. Not everything, though, was that old. Mr Potato Head was a definite product of the times.

Before becoming a popular child's toy in 1950s Britain, Mr Potato Head had to go through a few birth pangs in America. He was the brainchild of inventor and designer George Lerner. The idea, which he came up with in 1949, was that if children were given plastic parts of a face and body – noses, mouths, eyes, hats, arms, feet and the like – all with spikes on them, they could build a series of characters by attaching the various bits to vegetables, a potato being the most obvious. In a country still suffering food shortages following the Second World War, the idea met with some resistance. So Lerner sold the idea to a breakfast cereal company, who gave the face and body parts as prizes in its cereal boxes. In 1951, an

Mr Potato Head as he is today. In the 1950s his head would have comprised a real potato.

American toy manufacturing and distribution company saw the potential of Mr Potato Head, bought the rights and began manufacturing the toy themselves, paying Lerner a royalty for every one sold. Mr Potato Head became the subject of the first television advertisement to be aimed at children and what was essentially a very simple toy became a huge success.

Mr Potato Head arrived in Britain in 1952 and was soon joined by other vegetable-based friends. The toy is still popular today, although modern sets include a plastic potato-shaped body with holes for the body part spikes. In 2021, the current manufacturers, in a rebranding exercise, dropped the word 'Mr' from the name of the toy to make it more all-inclusive.

More toys of the 1950s

Here are just some of the many other toys that proved popular in the 1950s.

- John Bull Printing Outfits: One of Britain's oldest and most popular toys began with the establishment of its manufacturer, the Charter Stamp Company, in 1922. The toy, which came in several different outfit sizes, comprised rubber back-to-front letters that could be

A small John Bull Printing outfit, popular in the 1950s.

assembled, using small tweezers, in a wooden frame from right to left in order to make words and sentences. These were then pressed into an ink pad found in a small metal box and stamped onto paper. It was the company's proud boast that everything in a John Bull Printing Outfit, from the rubber letters to the cardboard box the kit came in, was made in the British Isles.

- Silly Putty: An engineer working at General Electric was in the process of putting boric acid and silicone rubber together when some of the strange substance he had created fell on the floor and bounced. There didn't seem to be any real scientific use for what he had discovered, so it was marketed as a toy. Once removed from the cartons in which it was sold, silly putty, as it became known, could be stretched and moulded and, left alone, very slowly flowed like liquid. It had no real use, but thousands of children found it fascinating.

- Play-Doh: These days available in a range of bright colours, Play-Doh was originally sold only in a shade of off-white. It was a modelling clay, originally invented in 1956 as a non-toxic wallpaper cleaner, but soon found more popularity as a toy.

- Hula-hoops: There was nothing new about hoops as toys. Children had been playing with them for many years, but chiefly as a toy that was stood on its rim and struck with a stick to bowl it along the road. But in 1958, the hoop went through a new incarnation, sold in bright colours and used by skilled children who taught themselves to swivel their hips to rotate the hoop around their bodies.

- Yo-yo: Two equally weighted discs were joined in the centre by a short spindle around which string was wound. The yo-yo could be made to fall and rise along the string as several clever tricks were performed during its decent, its time spinning at the bottom of the string and its climb back to the top. Although originally introduced in the 1930s, the yo-yo became immensely popular in school playgrounds of the 1950s.

- Diablo: A top comprised of two cone-shaped components joined at the pointed ends was placed on a length of string attached to two sticks, one held in each hand. By manipulating the sticks the top could be made to run along the string, tossed into the air and caught again while performing other tricks.

- Pick-up sticks: Forty-one short coloured sticks were spread on a table or the floor, as the players used two of the sticks to pick up the rest, in a particular order or by specific colour. The name of the game also became the title of a piece of music composed by jazz musician Dave Brubeck and recorded on his iconic long-playing record *Time Out* in 1959.

Bayko, Brickplayer and Dinky Builder building sets as advertised in the 1950s.

• Building sets: Unlike Meccano, which was essentially aimed at engineering projects, several companies of the 1950s made building sets for putting together model houses, garages, railways stations, etc. Bayko was one of the most popular. Its name was derived from Bakelite, one of the first forms of commercial plastic and from which the Bayko set parts were originally made. To erect a building, rods were first inserted into a base, then bricks, doors, windows and other parts were slotted between them to make walls, after which a roof was added. Originally produced in the 1930s, Bayko sets reached a peak in the 1950s when the right to manufacture the toy was acquired by Meccano Ltd

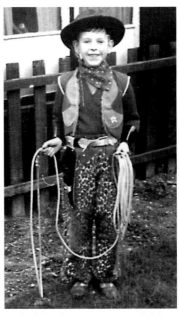

Cowboy outfits were among the more popular dressing-up outfits for boys.

Not just cowboy outfits, but model guns and more were all for sale to children of the 1950s.

Clockwork toys available from Tri-ang.

Magic sets were popular among aspiring magicians and conjurers.

and new parts were added to make the model buildings as realistic as possible. The other big modelling toy was Brickplayer, which used small bricks, along with an adhesive that was used like mortar to construct buildings exactly the way a real bricklayer might. When the

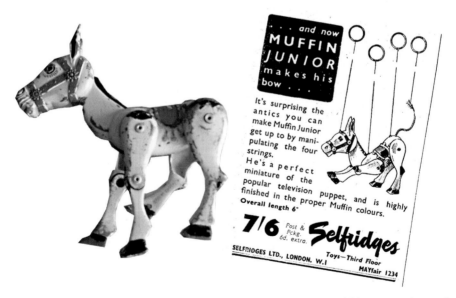

Muffin the Mule, a favourite children's television character, was available as a simple metal marionette.

model was finished, it could be soaked in warm water to dissolve the adhesive and free up the bricks for making another building. The size of the bricks meant that finished models were to scale with '0' gauge model railways.

All of these toys together make up only a part of what children played with in the 1950s. Equally popular were model boats, model aeroplane kits, bikes, boxes of magic tricks, chemistry sets, dressing up clothes (particularly cowboys), model steam engines, all kinds of clockwork toy, snapshot cameras with film developing outfits, model soldiers, model farmyards, glove puppets and marionettes, and a great variety of toy weapons that included spud guns that shot hard pellets of raw potato, bows and arrows that shot arrows with rubber suckers on the end (often removed by the brave), catapults with strong rubber that could shoot potentially lethal stones, and even – for older boys, at least – air rifles and pistols. Health and safety among toymakers of the 1950s wasn't what it is today.

Chapter 5

A Tonic for the Nation

Festival of Britain – Festival Exhibition – Skylon – Dome of Discovery – pavilions and displays – Battersea Pleasure Gardens – what remains of the Exhibition

FACT BOX

- The 1951 Festival Exhibition was inaugurated by the Labour Party and condemned by the Conservatives.
- The exhibition covered 27 acres on the south bank of the river Thames.
- Bright colours were chosen for exhibition buildings in contrast to the drabness of London buildings at the time.
- The main emblem of the exhibition was the Skylon, which resembled a 300ft space rocket.
- The exhibition was designed to be viewed in a specific order.
- The centre point of the exhibition was the Dome of Discovery, 83 feet high with a diameter of 365 feet.
- The Royal Festival Hall is all that remains today of the Festival Exhibition.

The austerity and bureaucracy prevalent at the start of the 1950s meant that few families had much to look forward to or to inspire them. The Festival of Britain was planned to change all that. It was generally agreed that it would become – and would be remembered as – a tonic for the nation.

It began with a letter to *The Times* newspaper in which an industrial design consultant reiterated an idea that had originated with the Royal Society of Arts. The suggestion was to organise an exhibition in 1951 to celebrate the centenary of The Great Exhibition of 1851. That earlier exhibition, which took place at the specially constructed Crystal Palace in London's Hyde Park, had been organised to display the wonders of

Crowds gather at the entrance to the Crystal Palace, venue for The Great Exhibition of 1851 and inspiration for the 1951 Festival Exhibition.

industry from every civilised country in the Victorian world. A new exhibition, a hundred years later, it was suggested, would provide the ideal opportunity to improve trade, show off British inventiveness, gain prestige and stand as an all-round boost to people's morale. The idea was swiftly taken up by the *News Chronicle* newspaper, which urged the President of the Board of Trade to see the scheme as an opportunity to stimulate British exports. Continuing the campaign for an exhibition, the *News Chronicle* focused also on international diplomacy and world unity. All of this happened in the face of a country whose people had seen the advent of the atomic bomb that effectively ended the Second World War, then the emerging division between countries of the East and West, leading to a perceived need for Britain to develop some kind of atomic programme of its own. So the calls for a national celebration of all things British were conceived during a climate of austerity, severe lack of everyday luxuries, a worsening international climate and a general underlying public paranoia.

Back in 1945, Conservative Party Prime Minister Winston Churchill, who had guided Britain through the Second World War and was regarded by many as the inspirational voice behind the country's victory, was

Above: the Skylon and Dome of Discovery. Below: the Royal Festival Hall, Skylon and Dome of Discovery seen across the Thames at night.

The official Festival guide to the exhibition, price half a crown (two shillings and sixpence).

surprisingly swept aside in a general election that put the Labour Party into power with Clement Attlee as the new Prime Minister. Attlee was swift to see the advantages of putting together the proposed project. It was to be called The Festival of Britain: A Land and its People. Although

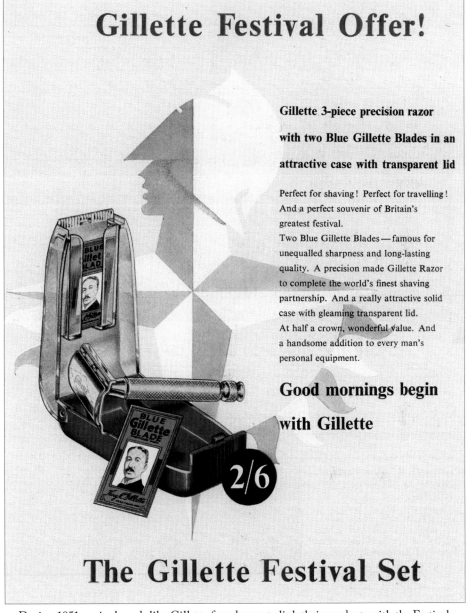

Gillette Festival Offer!

**Gillette 3-piece precision razor
with two Blue Gillette Blades in an
attractive case with transparent lid**

Perfect for shaving! Perfect for travelling!
And a perfect souvenir of Britain's
greatest festival.
Two Blue Gillette Blades — famous for
unequalled sharpness and long-lasting
quality. A precision made Gillette Razor
to complete the world's finest shaving
partnership. And a really attractive solid
case with gleaming transparent lid.
At half a crown, wonderful value. And
a handsome addition to every man's
personal equipment.

Good mornings begin
with Gillette

2/6

The Gillette Festival Set

During 1951, major brands like Gillette found ways to link their products with the Festival.

conceived as a celebration of all things British to be organised throughout
the whole of Britain, the centrepiece of the event was always planned to
be the amazing Festival Exhibition in London.

The design of the exhibition

Postage stamps issued at the time of the exhibition.

South of the river Thames at Lambeth, a 27-acre site, sitting between Waterloo Bridge and Westminster Bridge, untouched since a bombing raid during the Second World War, was chosen as the exhibition site. All that had survived the bombings were old Victorian buildings and railway sidings, and these were demolished to make way for the exhibition. A relatively young architect, Hugh Casson, was appointed as the Festival's Director of Architecture. With Casson at the helm, other young architects were brought in to begin work on a scheme that would showcase the principles of a new urban design, soon to feature in the

A souvenir mirror displaying the Festival logo.

rebuilding of much of Britain and specifically London in these post-war years.

The Festival of Britain had its own emblem seen on every printed brochure, pamphlet, catalogue, sign and souvenir around the exhibition. The emblem was designed by Abram Games, an official war poster artist

Aerial view of the Festival Exhibition with the Royal Festival Hall on the left of Hungerford Bridge and the Dome of Discovery dominating the opposite side of the exhibition site.

who was demobbed in 1946, and who was one of twelve artists invited to submit designs to the Arts Council and the Council for Industrial Design. His winning design depicted the head of Britannia wearing a crested helmet at the top of a compass-like star, with festive bunting hanging in a semi-circle from the left and right points of the star and incorporating the year 1951. The whole thing was designed in the traditional red, white and blue of the Union Flag.

All the buildings and any outdoor furniture planned for the exhibition were painted in bright colours, a stark contrast with most London buildings that had been blackened by the smoke of coal fires in every home and office. The layout of the exhibition presented something new, comprising a series of sequences arranged in a particular order to build into one complete story, rather in the way that chapters build into a complete book. It was the first exhibition of any comparable size to be designed as a kind of flowing narrative. For this reason, visitors were

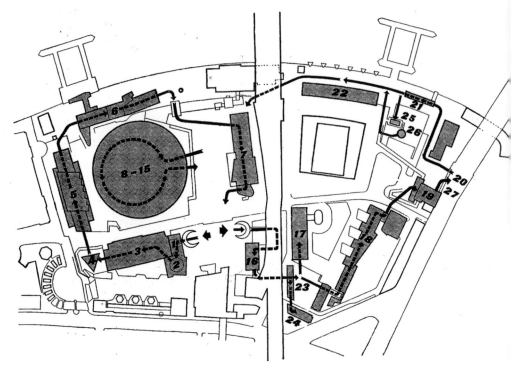

The way to go round the exhibition, as outlined in the brochure.

encouraged to follow a specific route around the exhibition site. A series of pavilions and displays were erected along the route, each telling its own story, and if each pavilion could be thought to represent a chapter in a book, so the exhibits within the pavilions – which again needed to be viewed in the right order – might represent paragraphs within each chapter. The organisers were keen to let people know they were welcome to start at the end and progress through the exhibition to the start, or to zigzag between the exhibits as they wished. But, it was emphasised, to do so might leave visitors feeling mystified by certain exhibits, not having had the benefit of information from what should have gone before.

The exhibition organisers were quick to recognise that walking around such a huge area would be exhausting, which is why plenty of places to eat and drink were included in the exhibition plans. There were twelve restaurants scattered around the exhibition site, each with its own small garden, where visitors could sit in the open air. Eating, drinking and general refreshment places included The Rocket, Fairway Café, The Dairy Bar, The Whistle, The '51 Bar, The Skylark, The Regatta

The '51 Bar beside the Thames.

Restaurant, Turntable Café, The Unicorn, The Garden Café, Thames-Side Restaurant and the Harbour Bar. Drinking fountains and ice cream kiosks were also scattered around the site.

Before the exhibition opened, there was only one tree on the South Bank site. By the time of the opening, more than sixty had been planted including water elms, maples, limes, poplars, whitebeams, birches, a catalpa and a turkey oak. Shrubs and plants were arranged in boxes, along with small artificial lakes and water fountains.

Viewed by walking through the exhibition in the suggested order, a story was created beginning in the past, continuing into the present and ending with a preview of the future. Interwoven throughout these three phases was the main theme of the exhibition: Britain's Land and its People. The land was represented by the country's scenery, climate and resources, which it was suggested were more varied than any other country of its size. The people, it was said, might not exhibit individual characteristics, but when taken together could not be mistaken for any other nation in the world. Throughput the entire exhibition, the underlying theme was the way the impact of Britain's land influenced its people and, in turn, the achievements people had made from their relationship with the land. It was hoped that visitors would pick up on the way the exhibition had

The Fairway fountains beside the river.

a story to tell, not so much in words, but in tangible things that made Britain the country it was at that time.

With the boundaries of the exhibition site falling between Waterloo and Westminster bridges, it also surrounded Hungerford Railway Bridge, which, in its position between the two other bridges, effectively divided the site in two. Rather than allow that to disturb the continuity of the exhibition's story, Hungerford Bridge was used as a natural dividing line

Entrance to the Dome of Discovery.

The Skylon, standing beside the Dome of Discovery.

The shape of the Skylon was copied to make a souvenir Biro ballpoint pen.

between the exhibition's two main narratives. The semi-circle of pavilions arranged upstream between Hungerford and Westminster bridges told the story of the land of Britain. The second semi-circle of pavilions arranged downstream between Hungerford and Waterloo bridges told the story of the people.

For the sum of 9*d*, children could make their own model of the Skylon.

Standing alone on the upstream side of Hungerford Bridge and dominating the Land Circuit, stood the exhibition's most impressive pavilion. It was called the Dome of Discovery and at that time it was the largest dome in the world, 83 feet high with a diameter of 365 feet. Inside, the Dome was dedicated to the discoveries, the developments and achievements of British men and women in mapping and charting the world, exploring the heavens and investigating the structure and nature of the universe. On the other side of Hungerford Bridge, standing at the centre of the People Circuit, there was the Royal Festival Hall, a concert hall for every type of entertainment, although orchestral concerts would be its dominant feature then and for the future.

The other major icon of the exhibition was the Skylon, which stood on the riverbank between Hungerford and Westminster bridges. *The Illustrated London News*, in its special Festival issue of 12 May 1951, described it like this:

> A beacon of light piercing upwards into the sky beckons visitors from far and near to the great Festival of Britain Exhibition on the South Bank of the Thames. This beacon is illuminated internally by a series of lamps grouped in clusters of three at frequent intervals round a central steel tube. Burnished aluminium cones reflect the light on to external reflectors. How very different will be the London scene by night this Festival summer when compared to the long nights of darkness that have preceded it.

The Skylon took its name from a combination of the words 'sky-hook' and 'nylon', and resembled a slender, 300-foot high space rocket, pointed at each end. The lower point rested in the centre of three cables strung from a three-legged structure below. From this, three more cables stretched up to support the centre of the structure. The cables were thin and practically invisible from a distance, giving the impression that the Skylon was floating in mid-air. Critics said it represented the state of Britain at that time, in that it had no visible means of support.

Opening day

The Festival Exhibition was officially opened on Thursday, 3 May 1951, a date no doubt chosen in anticipation of a fine spring day. It rained for most of the day. The opening ceremony was performed by King George VI who attended with other prominent members of the Royal Family, including Princess Elizabeth who, less than a year later, would be Queen. Also present were Prime Minister Clement Attlee, Leader of the Opposition Winston Churchill and other important members of

Both sides of a London Transport Festival bus ticket, issued during the Festival.

the Government. The opening ceremony was preceded by a Service of Dedication in St Paul's Cathedral, led by the Archbishop of Canterbury, who said: 'We determine to be joyful for a season and to renew our strength and spirit.' The opening ceremony was performed by the King standing on a specially built podium located outside on the steps of the cathedral. Broadcasting to the nation, he said: 'This is no time for despondency, for I see this Festival as a symbol of Britain's abiding courage and vitality.'

Following the official opening, forty-one gun salutes were fired from the Tower of London and Hyde Park, as members of the Royal party made their way back to Buckingham Palace in a procession whose route was thronged with thousands of people. That evening, the King officially opened the Royal Festival Hall, followed by a service of dedication led by the Archbishop of Canterbury. After an interval, a concert of British music included works by Handel, Parry, Purcell, Elgar, Vaughan Williams and Arne, naturally including 'Rule Britannia'.

On the evening of the exhibition opening, about 5,000 young people gathered on a bombsite behind St Paul's Cathedral, where a bonfire was lit by one Boy Scout. The fire was fed by nearly 3 tons of wood gathered from around the East End of London. It attracted crowds of an estimated 10,000 people and was the signal for more than 2,000 more bonfires to be lit all around the country.

The next day, the Royal Family took a tour of the exhibition, visiting all the pavilions.

The Whit Monday bank holiday fell that year on 14 May. It was the coldest Whit Monday since 1916, but the bitter weather didn't keep the crowds away. At one point there was a queue 2 miles long to get through the turnstiles at the entrance to Battersea Pleasure Gardens. People also flocked to the north bank of the Thames to see the lights of the Festival across the water and, in that single day, attendance to the exhibition on the south bank reached 93,012. The same day, attendance at Battersea Fun Fair topped 75,860 people.

It was clear from the start that London's Festival Exhibition was going to be a resounding success.

Around the pavilions and displays

Let's take a trip around the exhibition in the way visitors might have enjoyed it any time between May and September 1951 …

Opening times are 10.30 am to 11.30 pm on weekdays and 12.30 pm to 11 pm on Sundays. There are seven gates into the exhibition and admission is five shillings during the morning, or four shillings from mid-afternoon. We'll enter through the Embankment Gate, which takes us into the Upstream Circuit.

Once inside, we see that this is the circuit that is dedicated to the land, and it is divided into seven pavilions. In *The Land of Britain* pavilion, we see how the land literally beneath our feet was created from prehistoric times to the present with references to changes of climate from the ice age onwards. It includes eras when parts of Britain were ravaged by volcanoes, when deserts and jungles covered the land and generally how the geography of the country changed over the course of around 70 million years. In *The Natural Scene* pavilion, life in fresh water, the wild lands of Britain, the downlands, birds, trees and grasses are all covered.

The *Sea and Ships* pavilion.

Then comes *The Country*, including details of farming, livestock, breeding, milk and mechanisation. *Minerals of the Island* examines coal, steel and other minerals. *Power and Production* looks at lighting, industry, research, machinery and commerce. For *Sea and Ships*, the emphasis is on the years before steam, modern propulsion, shipbuilding, fishing vessels

The *Power and Production* pavilion.

Outside the
Transport pavilion.

and special ships for special purposes. Finally, *Transport* deals with rail, road, sea and air travel.

The impressive and huge Dome of Discovery is next on our itinerary, and is well worth the extra five shillings it costs to get in. The Dome is divided into eight sections: *The Land* looks at how the British have always been keen on exploration. *The Earth* deals with geology, archaeology and mineral wealth. Then comes *Polar*, which outlines conditions in the Arctic and Antarctic, with demonstrations in a theatre area by men who have actually experienced environments in these regions. *The Sea* section is devoted to British discoveries by sea, including hydrography and science at sea. The natural progression from here is to *The Sky*, in which exploration above the surface of the earth is investigated with a look at weather forecasts and research into the ionosphere. *Outer Space* is explored by astronomy with a look at the planets via telescope technologies. *The Living World* follows and, rather than looking at aspects of the planet, looks instead at the processes of nature, considering early biologists, Charles Darwin and modern research. Finally, *The Physical World* examines how matter is made, illustrated by chemical discovery, physical discovery and Britain's pioneering work in nuclear research.

Passing under Hungerford Bridge, heading towards Waterloo Bridge we now enter the Downstream Circuit, devoted to The People. Here we have six sections to enjoy. They begin with *The People of Britain*, which looks at ancient cultures, the beginnings of agriculture, the emergence of Christianity and invaders that helped populate the country. *The Lion and the Unicorn* signifies the two main qualities of the British national character: realism and strength, as opposed to fantasy, independence and imagination. It does this by means of language and literature, eccentricities, British craftsmanship, an instinct for liberty and an all-round indefinable character. *Homes and Gardens* follows the British into their homes, looking at the functions of different rooms – the kitchen, the parlour, a bed-sitting room – as well as the role of children in the house, and home entertainment. Next comes *The New Schools*, unveiling the way education has been in the past and the way it is today as the result

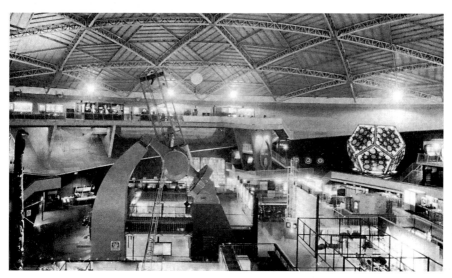

Inside the Dome of Discovery.

of the 1944 Education Act that empowered local education authorities to provide a full and efficient education for every child in Britain from the age of 5 to 15. *Health* is next on the itinerary, with displays helping people to learn more about their bodies, the importance of safe water, good drainage and the right food, biological standards, nursing, and penicillin as the century's most important discovery in clinical medicine. While the *Health* pavilion deals with people's physical well-being, the *Sport* pavilion next door concentrates on games and open-air recreation, pointing out how the British are so adept at inventing their own games, but also for adapting other people's. Our tour of the Downstream Circuit ends at the *Seaside*, or rather as good a representation of the British seaside as can be made on the banks of the Thames. Here visitors can look at the work of Britain's small ports, pleasure resorts and some of the wild stretches of undeveloped coasts around the British Isles.

Television in 1951 is still something of a novelty, so its representation in the exhibition attracts much interest. Strangely, this latest form of entertainment is on display in the *Transport* pavilion, where it is described as a method of sending moving pictures by radio. There is also a telecinema to visit, a 400-seat building that is the first of its type in the world, specially designed to show conventional films and television broadcasts, many in 3D with surround sound.

The seaside comes to the south bank of the Thames.

The Shot Tower that became part of the exhibition.

Nearby, the 1851 Centenary Pavilion displays a miniature model of the Crystal Palace, which, a century before, had housed The Great Exhibition that was the inspiration for the 1951 Festival Exhibition. Rotating screens at each end of the pavilion show views of The Great Exhibition with scenes of Queen Victoria at the opening ceremony, all accompanied by a collection of music that was played during the opening ceremony 100 years before.

One landmark around long before the Festival of Britain was conceived has now become part of the exhibition. The Shot Tower was built in 1826 for the purpose of manufacturing lead shot balls. This was achieved by dropping molten metal from the melting chamber at the top of the tower, which formed perfect spheres as it cooled in its 120-foot fall inside the tower. For the exhibition the tower has been transformed into a lighthouse whose beam flashes from sunset until the exhibition closing time.

Contrapuntal Forms, the sculpture that once stood outside the Dome of Discovery, survived the demolition of the exhibition and for many years more stood on the edge of this housing estate in Essex. It was removed for cleaning in mid-2021.

Particularly impressive are the sculptures and other artwork from more than twenty of the country's best known artists and sculptors, commissioned specially for the exhibition. They include the monumental group by Barbara Hepworth called *Contrapuntal Forms* (a word used in music to describe two different tunes that are played or sung at the same time), standing on a podium outside the Dome of Discovery. Another Hepworth abstract sculpture stands in the Thames-Side Restaurant. Also on show are Henry Moore's sculptures near the *Country* pavilion – and Jacob Epstein's gilded bronze sculpture at the entrance to the *Homes and Gardens* pavilion.

The Festival Pleasure Gardens

The Festival Exhibition, while entertaining, was very much slanted towards education. The Festival Pleasure Gardens, a little way down the south bank of the river at Battersea, was dedicated to relaxation and fun. Visitors could travel between the two sites by river boats. A.P. Herbert,

The Battersea Pleasure Gardens guide, price 1s 6d.

novelist, playwright, poet and politician, summed it up well in a long and somewhat rambling poem that ended:

> So come to us by river and survey
> The Clock They Could Not Silence on the way.
> You think us Neroes, fiddling in the flame?
> We think we're Drakes – and this is a gallant game.
> Think what you will. We hoist the Flag of Fun.
> We bid you WELCOME – and we pray for the sun.

One of cartoonist Roland Emett's creations comes to life in Battersea Pleasure Gardens.

The Guinness Festival Clock.

Arriving by boat, passengers disembarked at the Pleasure Gardens Pier, to stroll through the Terrace Walk and along a narrow strip of parkland called Riverside. Nearby, the Tree Walk was just what its name suggested: a place where visitors could ascend into the higher branches of the trees to walk along a wooden catwalk among the branches 30 feet above the ground. The walk was best taken at dusk or at night with the lights of the Pleasure Gardens spread out below.

Back on the ground, a huge tower rose into the air topped by a luminous pineapple. Down the sides of the tower, golden balls descended, vanishing into a bowl of light at the base and reappearing at the top. This was the Fountain Tower, and it stood between two areas known as the Piazza, which led to a traditional funfair, and The Parade, which took visitors on a more entertaining journey.

One of the highlights along The Parade was the Guinness Festival Clock, which did far more than merely tell the time. As the clock struck, various animated figures leapt into life. The Guinness Zookeeper emerged from under a cupola that turned into an umbrella as he rang a bell; the Mad Hatter popped into view and went fishing; a big yellow sun began to revolve; an ostrich struggled out of a chimney; above it all a circle of strange creatures revolved beneath a many-bladed fan while a musical box tinkled away; and of course a large clock face in the middle of it all told the time. Further along the parade stood an amphitheatre, a grotto of caves, a volcanic pit and a waterfall. At the end of the parade, four red columns supported a huge golden ball. From here, moving under a row of hanging chandeliers, visitors entered The Grand Vista, where steps led down to lakes containing gushing fountains. Here too were arcades designed in the Chinese Gothic style, with shops, restaurants and teahouses.

Visitors who then wished to move on to the Fun Fair could do so by taking a trip by rail along the Far Tottering and Oyster Creek Railway, with engines and carriages designed by Rowland Emett, probably the most famous of all the cartoonists whose work regularly appeared in the satirical magazine *Punch*. There were three weirdly designed engines called *Neptune*, *Wild Goose* and *Nellie*. Between them, they transported thousands of passengers every hour on a journey that began at Far Tottering Station, taking in along the way, Mrs Bristow's Folly, Tottering Woods, two other stations called Loambarrow Bottom and Cloud Cuckoo Halt, then finally to Oyster Creek Station, where they disembarked for the Fun Fair.

FESTIVAL PLEASURE GARDENS

KEY

1 Pleasure Gardens Pier
2 Staff Restaurant
3 Fountain Tower
4 East Gate
5 Peter Pan Railway
6 Shops

7 Festival Clock
8 The Walk
9 The Music Pavilion
10 Mermaid Fountain
11 The Amphitheatre
12 Grotto
13 Punch and Judy

15 Riverside Theatre
16 Administration
17 West Gate
18 The Grand Vista
19 Lakeside Stage & Tent
20 Fountain Lake
21 The Pier Tower and Oscar Creek Railway

22 Giant Fernhouse and Fireworks
23 Dance Pavilion
24 Nestlé's Playland
25 The Band Stand
26 The Fun Fair
27 Dragon Ride

BARS

B1 Ranelagh Beer Garden
B2 Vauxhall Beer Garden
B3 Cremorne Beer Garden
R1 Pier Snack Bar

RESTAURANTS and Cafés

R 1 Pier Snack Bar
R 2 Pier Restaurant
R 3 Terrace Tea Shop
R 4 The Pavilion Buffet
R 5 The Riverside Rooms
R 6 Vista Tea House
R 7 Crescent Restaurant
R 8 Aviary Restaurant
R 9 Tuck Shop
R 10 Festival Fare
R 11 Session Buffet
R 12 Garden Buffet

Key
Coach
28 S.E Gate
29 Oyster Creek
30 Boating Pool
31 Big Dipper
32 The Pizza
33 Children's Zoo
34 Aviary
35 Flower Gardens
L Lavatories

RIVER THAMES

THE PARADE

TERRACE WALK

Map of the Pleasure Gardens at Battersea, from the official brochure.

THE FESTIVAL AROUND THE COUNTRY

While the Festival Exhibition was the focal point of the Festival of Britain, it was by no means the only place that the Festival was celebrated. It wasn't even the only place in London. Here are some of the other locations where celebrations took place around Britain in 1951.

Exhibition of Science: 4 May – 30 September. This took place at South Kensington and was designed to showcase advances in science by way of working models which developed its theme by the use of things that visitors could see and believe in.

Exhibition of Architecture: 3 May – 30 September. By visiting Poplar in East London, visitors took a pre-organised tour around the streets to experience the district's architecture. The tour took in two churches, several housing estates, schools and shopping centres. Visitors were invited to make comparisons between the good design of a new building, furnished in a modern style for the occasion, and an older house with its so-called bad design.

Exhibition of Industrial Power: 28 May – 18 August. The conquest of power was the theme of the most ambitious exhibition after London's Festival Exhibition. It took place in Glasgow. Over an exhibition area of 100,000 square feet, visitors saw the two main sources of power in Britain at that time, namely coal and water. The first of these was represented by a gigantic sculptured mural of a cliff of coal, which, at 105 feet long, was the largest piece of sculpture ever produced in Scotland. The second power was represented by 20,000 gallons of water that cascaded over the roof of the glass tunnel that led visitors into an exhibition of hydroelectricity, civil engineering and irrigation.

Ulster Farm and Factory Exhibition: 1 June – 31 August. Taking place at Castlereagh, a suburb of Belfast, this told the story of the way the region earned its living though agriculture and industry.

Land Travelling Exhibition: May – October. If people could not go to the Festival exhibition in London, this was an attempt to bring important aspects of the exhibition to them. It comprised about 3,000 objects, which were carried on a fleet of lorries to four sites at Manchester, Leeds, Birmingham and Nottingham. Where premises were available and large enough, the exhibition was mounted for visitors to attend indoors. Where no premises were available, a structure made up of 100,000 square feet of canvas was erected for the purpose outdoors.

Sea Travelling Exhibition: May – October. HMS *Campania* was a former aircraft carrier that had seen service in the Second World War. In 1951, the ship became a miniature replica of the London Festival Exhibition which was taken to ten sites around the country. The floating exhibition visited Southampton, Dundee, Newcastle, Hull, Plymouth, Bristol, Cardiff, Belfast, Birkenhead and Glasgow.

The Fun Fair included rides with names like Three Abreast Gallopers, Lighthouse Slip, Leaping Lena, The Octopus, The Whip, Dodgem Cars, The Waltzer, Moon Rocket, The Ghost Train, Fly-O-Plane, The Rotor, Boomerang, Flying Cars, The Sky Wheel … and many more.

Other delights of the Pleasure Gardens included a children's zoo, a bird sanctuary, flower gardens, a dance pavilion, Punch and Judy shows, a puppet theatre, a children's play land and Peter Pan's Railway. Acrobatic displays that went on all day included performers who balanced on a spinning platform 60 feet above ground, others performing on a revolving wheel, more acrobats who performed on motorbikes and the Television Mast Man, who enacted his tricks at 140 feet above the ground. At night, there were huge firework displays, sponsored by all the big firework makers of the day.

Battersea Pleasure Gardens were open from 3 May, when the Festival Exhibition opened, until 3 September 1951. A funfair remained on the site until 1974.

After the exhibition

The Festival had never been without its critics, and its government sponsorship led to outcries from many who felt in a time of such austerity the money would have been better spent on housing for those who had lost their homes during the Second World War. Nevertheless, the exhibition was a resounding success as 8.5 million paying visitors flocked to London during the nearly five months that it was open.

The Festival Exhibition closed on 30 September 1951, and, almost immediately, work began on its demolition. By October, only a few weeks after its closure, the Conservatives returned to power with Winston Churchill as Prime Minister. The incoming government saw the Festival Exhibition as part of the misguided ideals of the previous Labour government, and viewed it, not as the successful event it turned out to be, but more as a symbol of financial mismanagement. For them, it became politically important to sweep away all traces of the exhibition as soon as possible. Exhibition landmarks like the Dome of Discovery and the Skylon, which might have gone on to be used elsewhere in the country, were all broken up for scrap. Some of the more important sculptures did survive and were transferred to new sites, but a great many more disappeared.

Today, little remains of the Festival Exhibition other than the Royal Festival Hall, refurbished in 2005–07 and now a Grade II listed building. There are a couple of plaques on a flagpole and in the pavement of the Southbank that commemorate where the Skylon once stood. A stone lion that once stood at the top of the London Brewery, which was demolished to make way for the Royal Festival Hall, and which was moved to the entrance of Waterloo Station during the exhibition, now stands at end of Westminster Bridge. Occasionally you might spot the old Festival emblem on a pub sign, or high up on a building on London's Oxford Street, or even on drainpipes on the Poplar housing estate in East London, which was once part of the general Festival. Other than these few, slightly obscure and easily overlooked icons, the Festival of Britain and its magnificent Festival Exhibition are largely forgotten.

A stone lion that once stood at the top of the London Brewery, demolished to make way for the exhibition when it was moved to the entrance of Waterloo Station, now stands at the end of Westminster Bridge. It's one of the few things remaining from the Festival Exhibition.

Chapter 6

God Save the Queen

The coronation of Queen Elizabeth II – coronation fever and souvenirs – the procession and ceremony – importance of television

FACT BOX

- Coronation Day was Tuesday, 2 June 1953, and it rained.
- Queen Elizabeth was 25 when she came to the throne.
- The Queen was the first sovereign in 200 years to accede while abroad.
- Coronation celebrations were condemned by two Members of Parliament.
- News of the conquest of Everest hit the news headlines on Coronation Day.
- The Gold State Coach had been used for every coronation since 1821.
- The Queen's dress contained 1,333 diamonds and 169 pearls.
- The coronation was responsible for a huge increase in television sales.

Tuesday, 2 June 1953: Coronation Day. As officially the second day of summer, it was thought that there might be a good chance of glorious weather for what was to be a joyous occasion. In fact, in the words of Air Ministry experts, the forecast was for 'a weather cocktail with nearly every ingredient but snow'. A senior forecaster at the Ministry told the *Daily Mirror* newspaper: 'There will be fresh or strong northerly winds, likely to be gusty with showers and short sunny intervals. Showers may be heavy at times with hail and possibly thunder.' It didn't stop the crowds, who turned out in their thousands. Two days before the coronation, The Mall – the long, straight road that leads from Trafalgar Square to Buckingham Palace, taking in Admiralty Arch on the way – was solid with cars crawling bumper to bumper as early as six o'clock in the morning, and this at a time when car ownership in Britain was low and roads were normally uncrowded. Many of those attending arrived in London a day or more in advance to claim their spot along the coronation route, sleeping rough on the pavements rather than losing their places.

Queen Elizabeth II acceded to the throne on the death of her father, King George VI, on 6 February 1952. She was in Kenya at the time, 25 years old and the first sovereign for 200 years to accede while abroad. Although tradition has it that the heir to the throne officially becomes the next monarch immediately on the death of the previous one, the time between her accession and coronation was sixteen months, largely due to the tradition of allowing an appropriate amount of time of mourning to pass before holding a major festival. It also gave adequate time for the complicated process of planning a coronation.

There was nothing sinister or political, as is sometimes suggested, about the length of time between Queen Elizabeth's accession and coronation. The fact that her father's coronation took place a mere five months after his accession was because King George VI simply took over the plans that were in the process of being made when his brother, King Edward VIII, chose to abdicate before his own coronation could take place. The time between Kind Edward VIII's accession and his coronation was always planned to be eighteen months.

Coronation fever

In the weeks and months leading up to 2 June, Britain went mad with Coronation fever. Red, white and blue proliferated on everything, from the flags and bunting that people bought to hang from windows or string across streets, to the wrapping paper around loaves of sliced bread. Just as abundant were the colours gold and red. Bars of Nestlé chocolate added gold lettering to the red wrappers for which the brand was famous. Golden *E II R* inscriptions began appearing on the new pillar boxes, *ER* for *Elizabeth Regina*, the Roman figure *II* between the letters indicating that the new queen was the second Elizabeth in the history of Britain's monarchy. Biscuit tins, tobacco

By the time of the coronation, new post boxes were displaying the *E II R* insignia.

Coronation souvenirs proliferated. Clockwise from top left: coronation chocolate tin, tea caddy, lapel badge, spoon, mug, powder compact and pencils.

tins, chocolate boxes, china mugs, plates and jugs, cigarette lighters, penknives and all kinds of souvenir featured pictures of Her Majesty, with or without Prince Philip, always wearing her crown, inevitably with the date of the coronation that was burned into the minds of all, usually with slogans like *Long May She Reign* and *Long Live The Queen* added into the designs.

Not everyone saw the coronation as a reason to be celebrate, however. Two labour Members of Parliament in particular were outspoken in their condemnation of the whole thing. MP John Freeman had this to say: 'I do disapprove of the ceremony of establishing the head of the State in which we all have a share and using it as an occasion for glorification of every kind of anti-Socialist belief and every myth which can be found anywhere in our history.' MP Barbara Castle joined in: 'I hope it is the last coronation of this kind this country will ever see, utterly unrepresentative as it is of the Britain and the Commonwealth of the ordinary people.' Reminding the nation that the British were not normally known for big, brash celebrations in the way some other countries were, journalist William Connor, writing as Cassandra in the *Daily Mirror* on the

Souvenir issue of the *Daily Mirror* and *Sunday Pictorial*, containing newspapers for 28 May to 3 June, on sale on 4 June 1953, price 1*s*.

morning of Coronation Day, was quick to put them in their place: 'Stop putting the black crepe around these silly, soppy, crazy, lovable, islands that today and tomorrow are on the big binge for once in their solemn and not colourful lives.'

Children were particularly caught up in the fervour. At school, even the youngest were encouraged to learn about why there was so much celebration in the air, and to create artwork like friezes along walls of

Coronation street
decorations in
(top to bottom)
The Mall and
Fleet Street in
London and at
Southwold in
Suffolk.

Two coronation street parties, usually attended by children in fancy dress.

classrooms on which every child had the opportunity to paint or draw contributions to illustrate their ideas of the coronation procession and to perhaps border the whole thing with stamps showing the Queen's head. At home, they made coronation scrapbooks, pasting in pictures of the Queen from magazine articles and other coronation-related items like decorated sweet wrappers. Coach outings were organised for pupils to visit London in advance of the great day to see the street decorations, particularly those that lined The Mall.

Pop-up pages from a coronation book sold in association with the *Daily Express* newspaper.

On the day of the coronation, and for some days after, tables and chairs were brought out into the streets and filled with cakes and lemonade for children's street parties. Fancy dress was very often the order of the day.

New toys began to appear in the shops: models of the golden coach in which the Queen would ride and the horses that pulled it; kits to make your own coach model out of plastic to be painted gold or already coloured cardboard; pop-up books showing what the procession would look like, along with facts about the coronation; jigsaw puzzles depicting royal occasions; board games based on the procession route; and View-Master stereo viewers with special 3D views of the Queen and coronation. Children's comics published during Coronation Week inevitably featured their characters involved in coronation shenanigans. Korky the Cat, who appeared weekly on the front cover of *The Dandy*, for example, was seen to be painting his pillowcase red, white and blue, then sitting in it suspended on a string of flags strung across The Mall as he waved his own flags and the royal coach passed below.

The week before

On Wednesday, 27 May, the Queen and Prince Philip were driven to Westminster Abbey for the biggest so far of many coronation rehearsals. Undaunted by teeming rain, a crowd of about 5,000 gathered to watch as she was escorted under an umbrella into the Abbey. As she went inside, the crowd ran for cover. Then the rain stopped and they returned to see her emerge again sometime later.

That evening, a banquet in the Queen's honour was organised at Westminster Hall and attended by representatives from all the parliaments of the Commonwealth. A toast to the Queen was proposed by Australia's Minister of Labour Harold Holt, who called the Queen 'the radiant embodiment of hope to millions'. British Prime Minister Winston Churchill told the banquet's 750 guests: 'We feel that her Gracious Majesty here with us today has consecrated her life to all her peoples in all her realms. We are resolved to prove, on the pages of history, that this sacrifice shall not be in vain.'

On Thursday, 28 May, the Queen gave a garden party in the grounds of Buckingham Palace for about 7,000 Commonwealth guests who had arrived in London for the coronation. It was a blazing hot day.

That evening, it was reported that the Queen had completed writing the speech she was due to broadcast by radio on Coronation Night. With some advice from Prince Philip, it was said she had written every word herself – in pencil. From the start, she had commanded: 'The words I speak shall be my own words, and from my heart, even if they are not the words of a practised writer.' In the broadcast she made on the evening of the coronation, she said: 'I am sure this, my coronation, is not the symbol of power and a splendour that are gone but a declaration of our hopes for the future, and for the years I may, by God's grace and mercy, be given to reign and serve you as your Queen.'

On Friday, 29 May, the Queen attended a final full-scale rehearsal of the coronation ceremony, when waiting crowds had the opportunity to see some of the dresses that would be worn on the day by the Maids of Honour. In the evening, along with Prince Philip and Princess Margaret the Queen attended an all-night pre-coronation ball, given by her Household Brigade at Hampton Court Palace. She was cheered on by about 20,000 people who had gathered outside Buckingham Palace, more crowds along the route and then a cheering crowd of about 30,000 outside the Hampton Court Palace gates.

On Sunday, 31 May, the Queen and Prince Philip attended a service in the Queen's Chapel at Marlborough House. When they returned to Buckingham Palace an estimated 30,000 people were there ready to cheer, while police, both mounted and on foot, tried their best to hold them back.

On Monday, 1 June, the Queen presided over a luncheon party at Buckingham Palace for Commonwealth leaders, while in the wet and rainy streets of London, the crowds gathered and prepared to bed in for the night, ready for the next day.

The day of the coronation and the day after: anticipated on the 2 June front page of the *Daily Mirror* newspaper and reported on the front page of 3 June.

The day of the coronation dawned and the morning newspapers were full of stories about … the conquest of Everest. On 29 May, during an expedition led by Colonel John Hunt, Edmund Hillary, from New Zealand, and Tenzing Norgay, a Nepalese Sherpa, became the first to reach the summit of Mount Everest, the world's highest mountain. The news had been brought by a Sherpa runner from the Everest base camp and radioed to Kathmandu, the news finally arriving in Britain on the eve of the coronation. The Queen sent a telegram to the British Minister in Kathmandu. It stated: 'Please convey to Colonel Hunt and all members of the British expedition my warmest congratulations on their great achievement in reaching the summit of Mount Everest – Elizabeth R.' The story featured fairly prominently in all the daily newspapers, which were otherwise dominated by coronation news.

The procession

The Queen and Prince Philip rode from Buckingham Palace to Westminster Abbey in the Gold State Coach that had been used at the

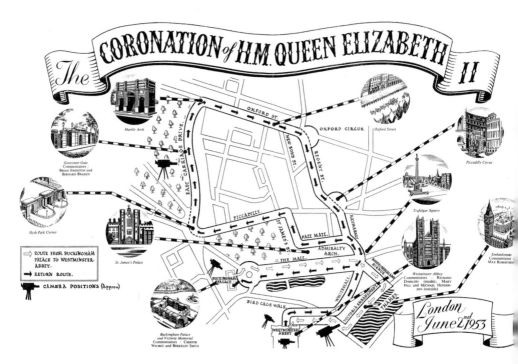

The route taken to and from Westminster Abbey.

coronation of every British monarch since George IV in 1821. The coach was commissioned in 1760 and completed in 1762 at a cost of £7,562. It was 24 feet long, 12 feet wide, gilded with gold and decorated with carvings and painted panels by Italian painter and engraver Giovanni Battista Cipriani. The interior was lined with velvet and satin. The coach was pulled by a team of eight grey gelding horses named Cunningham, Tovey, Noah, Tedder, Eisenhower, Snow White, Tipperary and McCreery.

The State Coach travelled at the centre of a huge procession. In front of the coach, on foot and horseback, the procession included detachments of the Royal Artillery, representatives of the Armed Forces, War Office

Coronation ephemera, including invitations, passes, letters, instructions on how to dress for the event and bound copies of the order of service.

staff, members of the Air Force and Army councils, Admiralty sea lords, Yeomen of the Guard and the Massed Bands of the Household Cavalry. Behind the coach, also on foot and horseback, but also in their own carriages, came royal dukes, equerries, the Lord Chamberlain, the Keeper of the Queen's Purse, various pages and many other officials.

The Queen's dress was designed by leading British fashion designer Norman Hartnell. It was made of satin with emblems of the United Kingdom and the Commonwealth embroidered in gold and silver thread. On her head she wore the George IV State Diadem, the crown she was

Accompanied by the Duke of Edinburgh, the Queen sets out for Westminster Abbey.

"If it rains, we've had it."

"Oh. stop nagging, they'll be dry by Tuesday"

" It's Parliament Square for you lot—and 14 days C.B. for anyone I catch
winking to the Television Cameras !"

"Did you hear that?
It cheered!"

How cartoonists saw the big day.

depicted wearing on British postage stamps. It featured roses, shamrocks
and thistles, with 1,333 diamonds and 169 pearls. The Queen's procession
was made up of 250 people, including church leaders, Commonwealth
prime ministers, members of the Royal Household, civil leaders, military
leaders and the Yeoman of the Guard. The processional route was a short
one: from the Palace, along The Mall, into Northumberland Avenue,
then along the Victoria Embankment and so to the Abbey.

After the ceremony, processing out of the Abbey, the Queen again
boarded the Gold State Coach for the ride back to Buckingham Palace,
this time by a longer journey that passed the throngs of cheering crowds.
The route left Westminster Abbey and travelled down Whitehall, around
Trafalgar Square into Pall Mall, then Piccadilly, turning into East

THE CEREMONY

Queen Elizabeth II was the thirty-ninth sovereign to be crowned in Westminster Abbey, the location for coronations since 1066. The service began at 11.15 am with the Queen being escorted into the Abbey by Officers of State. When she reached the Chair of Estate, the ceremony commenced, presided over by the Archbishop of Canterbury and lasting nearly three hours. It was divided into six parts:

The Recognition was the formal acknowledgement of Queen Elizabeth as Queen. She stood by her chair and faced, in turn, all four corners of the Abbey as the congregation expressed their homage with cries of 'God save Queen Elizabeth'.

Taking the Oath involved the Queen promising that she would rule her peoples always according to law, justice and mercy.

The Anointing was carried out by the Archbishop of Canterbury who made the sign of the cross in holy oil on the head and hands of the Queen in order to make a spiritual preparation for the crowning. This part of the ceremony took place as the Queen removed her state robe and sat for the first time in the Coronation Chair of Edward I.

The Presentation and Investiture was when the Queen received the State Regalia. First she took the Golden Spurs and Jewelled Sword of State, which she offered to the altar. Next the Orb was handed to her as a symbol of the sovereignty of Christianity. The Coronation Ring, the sign of Royal Dignity, was then placed on the fourth finger of her right hand. Finally, she received the Sceptre with the Cross and the Sceptre with the Dove.

The Crowning was carried out by the Archbishop of Canterbury with the Queen seated in the Coronation Chair, wearing a mantle of purple and gold braid. The crown was a representation of the principal symbol of sovereignty. The crowning was heralded by a fanfare of trumpets and cries of 'God save the Queen'. At the same moment, a salute of guns was fired at the Tower of London.

The Inthronisation was when the Queen proceeded to her throne, while the Archbishop counselled her to 'Stand firm and hold fast from henceforth the seat and state of royal and imperial dignity'. Still on her throne she received the homage of princes and peers, beginning with Prince Philip. The coronation ceremony was concluded by an anthem and the sounding of trumpets.

Following the ceremony, the Queen proceeds to the West Door of the Abbey.

Carriage Drive then turning again into Oxford Street, along Regent Street and Haymarket, once again around Trafalgar Square, under Admiralty Arch, along The Mall and through the Palace gates.

That night, at 9.45 pm, the Queen came onto the balcony of Buckingham Palace to switch on the floodlights that lit up ornate arches and other decorations along The Mall. The crowds that lined the long road from Trafalgar Square to the Palace gates were shoulder to shoulder, waiting for another appearance. At 10.30 pm, the Queen returned to the balcony, then again at 11.30 pm and midnight. Coronation Day was over.

Televising the coronation

The coronation was responsible for more people buying or renting televisions than ever before. Yet, if early plans had come to fruition, the pubic would have seen very little of the ceremony. The first problem was lack of transmitters needed to transmit a signal nationwide. In 1951, the Government, concerned about a new conflict with Germany and the onset of the Cold War, had diverted money away from the building of transmitters and into rearmament. By 1952, when planning for the coronation began in earnest, there were still large swathes of Britain, especially along the coasts, that could not receive a television signal. The second problem was that the Queen did not enjoy being televised. Cameras had been banned from Westminster Abbey for her wedding to Prince Philip in 1947, she refused to allow her Christmas message to be televised and she had asked the BBC not to dwell on her face during the televising of the Trooping of the Colour ceremony. Consequently, the Coronation Commission, chaired by Prince Philip, decreed that although cameras could be set up to record, from a safe distance, the procession into the Abbey, the actual ceremony could not. That same year, the Archbishop of Canterbury told reporters that the world would have been a happier place if television had never been discovered.

In October, things changed. The Coronation Commission was persuaded to change its mind and it was decided that televising of the important crowning ceremony would be allowed, providing there were no close-ups. With the decision taken, and with people flocking to obtain televisions, the Government was goaded into action to build new transmitters, some of them only temporary. In the end, an estimated 20.4 million viewers watched the coronation on about 2.7 million televisions, and that was just in their homes. Another 1.5 million or so were gathered in places like ballrooms, churches, town halls and hospitals which had been given collective licences to show the day on big screens. In the Royal Festival Hall, 3,000 ticket holders watched from 10 am and were given packed lunches as part of their ticket prices. A similar number filled the Odeon cinema in London's Leicester Square, while Butlin's Holiday Camps showed the day on large screens at Filey, Skegness and Clacton. As was a habit of many people at the time, there would also have been small crowds around the windows of electrical shops that sold televisions and which usually had a number of sets in the window, all working and – with only one channel to watch – inevitably tuned in to the live broadcast of the coronation.

The pictures of course were in black and white, since the first regular colour television broadcasts didn't begin until 1967. But in 1953, experiments were already underway and, on Coronation Day, 200 children at London's Great Ormond Street Hospital saw part of the procession in colour, thanks to three early forms of colour TV camera situated in Parliament Square, whose signals were sent to the hospital via a closed circuit system. More traditional black and white television cameras were positioned around the route of the procession and in Westminster Abbey.

The week before the big day, television began broadcasting build-up programmes. A cookery programme told viewers how to prepare melon cocktails and salmon mousse to eat in front of their televisions. Police officers gave advice on how to behave for those who intended to line the streets to see the procession, and how to prevent house burglaries while the whole family was gathered in one room watching television.

Television broadcasts began on the night before the coronation as cameras placed at the Victoria Memorial opposite Buckingham Palace showed the people already in position along The Mall and ready to spend the night there in order to get a good view of the procession the following day.

On the morning of 2 June, the day's television coverage was opened by popular announcer Sylvia Peters. Then the picture changed to show the Queen leaving Buckingham Palace and moving along The Mall with a surprisingly close view of her face at the window of the coach. As the journey progressed and new cameras took up the scene, the coach was televised on its journey to the Abbey. More cameras perched high on specially built stands and the roof of a nearby building recorded the Queen's entry into the Abbey. Inside, in a cubicle perched high on a gallery above the arches of the nave, veteran broadcaster Richard Dimbleby sat ready to commentate on the proceedings, side by side with another camera that stood at the ready, while another over the West Door was poised to survey the nave as the royal procession entered the building. In this way, every part of the service was recorded, before the procession left the Abbey to take the long route back to the Palace, followed all the way by the switching of cameras and commentators along the route. In all, eight BBC commentators – seven men and one woman – commentated on the day's proceedings.

Television coverage of the event ended at 5.20 pm that day with the last appearance of the Queen on the balcony of Buckingham Palace, but a good number of the population continued watching their sets, through the children's TV that followed, the rest of the evening's programmes and finally a summation of the day by Richard Dimbleby, broadcasting live from a now empty Westminster Abbey.

It would be another nine years before the first live television signal could be broadcast across the Atlantic to America, so Americans saw scenes of the coronation later than viewers in Britain – but not by much. America's two biggest TV companies, the Columbia Broadcasting System and the National Broadcasting Company, had flown their own camera teams to Britain to cover the day. In order to get pictures to American viewers on the same day, RAF Canberra planes, the world's fastest jet bombers, were mobilised. As soon as the crowning ceremony finished, films from the American crews plus telefilm from the BBC were sent by jet to New York. Then a second jet flew scenes of the procession through the streets to Buckingham Palace after the ceremony. By 11 pm UK time, which translated as 6 pm on the east coast of America, 70 million Americans were seeing the first of the day on 70 million televisions.

Remembering the coronation

By Saturday, 6 June, a full-length colour film of the coronation, the processions and the crowning ceremony inside Westminster Abbey was ready to be shown on a new wide screen at the Odeon cinema in London's Leicester Square. The film went on general release throughout Britain on 7 June.

But it was another rather sentimental though nevertheless evocative film released two whole years later that won the hearts of many. It was called *John and Julie* and it told the story of two children, Julie, who is at a boarding school, and her older friend John, who lives locally. Both decide to run away to London to see the Queen and watch the coronation. The story, filmed in colour rather than the more traditional black and white of this era, follows their journey to London, some amusing adventures along the way and finally Coronation Day, which they watch courtesy

Cinema poster for the film *John & Julie*, about two children who ran away from home to see the coronation.

of actual film footage of the day edited into the story. It ends as Julie, helped through the crowds to the gates of Buckingham Palace, presses her face up against the railings and gets her wish to see the Queen as she comes out on the Palace balcony. The film not only sums up just what was so good and patriotic about the coronation, but also gives a glance into a now forgotten view of what the country in general, and London in particular, was like in the 1950s.

Chapter 7

Shops, Shopping and Shoppers

Second-hand shops – grocers – greengrocers – sweet shops – tobacconists – fishmongers – the rise of the supermarkets

FACT BOX

- Post-war rationing of food and other items lasted until 1954.
- Most shops were privately owned.
- Sweet shops sold cigarettes and other tobacco-based products.
- Many butchers hung raw meat on hooks in the street outside their shops.
- It was customary for mothers to leave prams and their babies outside shops while they went inside.
- The first British supermarket opened in London in 1951.

A typical high street of the 1950s in Scunthorpe.

Shoppers in the 1950s had no shopping malls or big chains of food-based supermarkets, although most decent sized towns did have branches of large chains like Marks & Spencer and Woolworth. Some of the smaller shops might also have had other branches in neighbouring towns. But by and large, shopping was carried out in privately owned shops, each catering for a different aspect of daily life, and whose produce only occasionally overlapped with that of other shopkeepers. It was a place where shop doors rang bells as they were opened to alert each shopkeeper to the arrival of a new customer, and those shopkeepers were dedicated to offering their customers the best service possible.

At the start of the 1950s, austerity measures and building regulations prevented shops from updating the look of their stores or the replacement of frontages unless special permission was granted by the Ministry of Works in 1951. The high street therefore looked very little different from the way it had looked before the outbreak of the Second World War, more than ten years previously.

It was common back then for a butcher's shop to display huge chunks of meat, often uncomfortably identifiable as part of an animal like a cow or pig, hanging on hooks in the street outside the shop, along with rabbits, complete from head to tail, all with flies buzzing around and doing

Meat hanging on hooks outside butchers' shop was commonplace in the 1950s.

A Woolworth store, decorated here for the coronation of King George VI in 1937 would have looked much the same until 1951, when stores were given permission to introduce some form of modernisation.

everything flies do when they alight on raw meat. The hooks on which they hung have become immortalised in cockney rhyming slang. If you hear someone today saying 'Let's have a butchers', the reference will be to a butcher's hook. In other words, 'Let's have a look'.

What other shops might be found on a 1950s high street? There was nearly always a toy shop, with windows surrounded by children sizing up what might be bought with next week's pocket money or, for larger, more expensive items, what might be wheedled out of parents and other relations for a birthday or Christmas present. Elsewhere, there was likely to be an undertaker, tastefully furnished and smelling of lilies; a launderette with coin-operated washing machines and tumble dryers; an electrical shop selling radios, more commonly referred to as wirelesses; a bicycle shop, maybe just branching out into motorbikes; a stationers, known for the quality of its fountain pens and second-hand typewriters; definitely a book shop, with new books at the front and a dusty, musty room full of second-hand books at the rear; a music shop that sold gramophone records alongside sheet music and musical instruments.

Other shops common in the 1950s included ironmongers, which sold items like nuts and bolts, door handles, hinges, in fact almost any small

A Wall's ice cream advertisement from 1951 with its rather romanticised view of a typical British shop of the time.

item made of metal, as well as paraffin, oil and tins of a strange gel-like substance guaranteed to clean just about anything off filthy hands. Then there were offal shops, which sold meat products that originated as animal organs like hearts, brains or livers; pie and mash shops, actually

RATIONING

Food shops were among the worst hit by rationing in the early years of the decade. The scheme had begun in January 1940, four months after the outbreak of the Second World War. Before the war, Britain imported something like 55 million tons of food from other countries. With the outbreak of war, as German submarines began attacking British supply ships, it became necessary to limit the amount of food the average person was allowed to buy each week.

A household representative, usually the wife, took the family's birth certificates to a central point, where she was issued

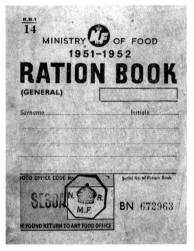

A ration book from the early 1950s.

with an identity card. Later, the identity card was used to release ration books, different colours for different members of the family. The books contained pages of small coupons which were cut out by shopkeepers in exchange for the basic necessities. A typical ration of food per week for a British adult during the war

DO NOT FILL IN ANYTHING ON THIS PAGE UNLESS you need to deposit with your retailer pages of COUPONS		
FOOD	NAME AND ADDRESS OF RETAILER WITH WHOM COUPONS ARE DEPOSITED.	INITIALS OF RETAILER.

NOTES
DEPOSITED ROWS OF COUPONS SHOULD BE RECOVERED AND PRODUCED TO THE FOOD OFFICE IF A TEMPORARY RATION CARD IS REQUIRED OR THE ADDRESS IS CHANGED.
WHERE THE ADDRESS IS CHANGED MAKE SURE THAT THE PARTICULARS GIVEN ON PAGE 6 ARE CORRECT BEFORE GOING TO THE FOOD OFFICE.

TO RETAILERS
It is essential for the successful operation of the rationing system that coupons should be either cancelled or cut out as appropriate, whenever rationed food is supplied to a consumer.

ENTER NAMES AND ADDRESSES OF RETAILERS

MEAT J. SAINSBURY LTD.,
46, HIGH STREET,
CAMBERLEY.

EGGS STOKES & SONS,
38, Park Street
CAM

FATS
L. & R. TOLLEY,
12, LONDON ROAD
CAMBERLEY

CHEESE
L. & R. TOLLEY,
LONDON ROAD
CAMBERLEY.

BACON
LONDON
CAMBERLEY

SUGAR
CAMBERLEY

SPARE 3

Inside the ration book, specific retailers were identified for each food product bought.

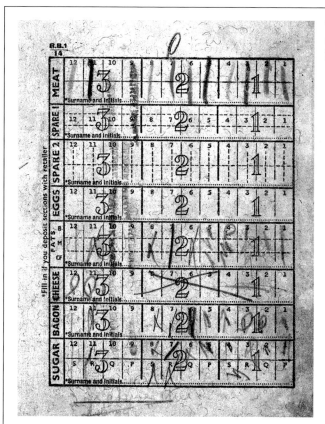

The back page of a typical 1950s ration book.

was 4 ounces of bacon or ham, 2 ounces of butter, 2 ounces of cheese, 4 ounces of margarine, 4 ounces of cooking fat, 3 pints of milk, 8 ounces of sugar, 2 ounces of tea and one fresh egg. The same adult was also allowed, 1 pound of preserves like jam or jelly every two months and 12 ounces of sweets every four weeks. Fruit and vegetables were not rationed, but were usually in short supply. Other commodities like petrol and even newly made furniture were also rationed.

By 1950, a little over four years after the war ended, although some restrictions were lifted, a lot of rationing continued. As late as 1952, sugar, butter, cheese, margarine, cooking fat, bacon, meat and tea were still on ration. Sugar rationing ended in 1953, and meat, the last commodity to be rationed, became freely available in 1954. It was, therefore, the food shops that were the worst hit.

small restaurants rather than retail outlets, where diners could partake of meat pies with mashed potatoes covered in a strange green liquor made from water left over from the preparation of stewed eels, coloured by the addition of parsley; and second-hand shops.

Buying a bargain

In the high streets of most major towns, or tucked away in side streets away from the town centre, depending how upmarket or downmarket their products might be, second-hand shops had something for every type of 1950s bargain hunter.

Some were little more than junk shops, with dust-covered window displays that had clearly not be changed for years, and interiors that were little better, places where bargain hunters convinced themselves they were going to find an overlooked and valuable artefact of some kind. Most came away dusty and disappointed. At the other end of the scale, more usually found in the better areas of a town, antique shops displayed genuine rarities of silverware, glass, maybe paintings, often jewellery and watches, highly priced but truly valuable. In between there were establishments that called themselves something like The Bargain Centre.

Such places were not posh enough to be called antique shops, but they were several steps higher than junk shops. They were where people came to sell unwanted household items to be sold on to others at a small profit for the shopkeeper. Inside, there was likely to be a lack of a counter of the type found in other shops, just shelves of fascinating paraphernalia, of which records, all stacked neatly in boxes under different categories – classical, pop, jazz, comedy – often played a big part. In the early years of the decade records were brittle, easily breakable, made of shellac and known as seventy-eights, after the number of revolutions per minute they made on the turntable. At the start of the decade there would have been a good number of those still around. Later, bargain centres and the like would more likely be found displaying LPs, short for long players, also known as thirty-threes, although their revolution rate per minute was actually thirty-three and a third. There were forty-fives too, smaller in diameter and faster on the turntable. The sixteen revolutions per minute found on some record players at that time never really caught on.

Records aside, stock found in bargain centre types of shop was likely to include things like toasters, teapots and table lamps; Monopoly boards, motor horns and mouth organs; watches, cameras, a bowler hat, a dressmaker's dummy, a sewing machine, a Bakelite hair dryer, all manner of toys, pictures, ornaments … in fact, anything someone wanted to sell and someone else was likely to buy.

Grocers

The grocer's shop on the corner of so many streets was the hub of the community. Inside, the grocer, who usually owned the business himself, would be dressed in a long white coat. He stood behind his counter and his grocery produce stood on shelves behind him. While rationing pervaded, it was likely that households would be registered with their own grocer, bought only from him and took what he had been told to offer. But as rationing relented, grocery items became more abundant.

Personal and friendly service from a local grocer.

Soap manufacturer J. Bibby of Liverpool was founded in 1830 and, by 1950, employed 5,000 people. The number of different types of soap they sold through grocers' shops was vast.

While he took a customer's needs off the shelves and laid them on the counter, a good grocer could often be heard going through a quiet liturgy of grocery items that his customer might have forgotten they wanted: 'Are you okay for sauce, gravy, soup, pickles, mustard, butter, lard, jam, marmalade? Do you need biscuits? We have custard creams, bourbon creams, fig rolls, chocolate digestives, garibaldi, ginger nuts, shortcake, pink wafers, jammy dodgers. How about soap? We have a dozen different types for all needs. Any meats today – bacon, ham, Spam, tongue?' Loose items would be weighed and slid into a brown paper bag and, with a turn of the wrist, the bag would be rotated a couple of times so that the ends were twisted, securing and sealing the contents before the bag was placed on the counter.

At the end of the counter stood the bacon slicer, a fearsome machine. A chunk of meat, especially ham or bacon, was placed on a stainless steel slab, spiked to keep it in place, and then pushed towards a huge circular blade. Turning a handle on the side of the machine set the blade into swishing motion as the meat advanced towards it to be sliced thick or thin, depending on the whim of the customer. There was talk of small boys who ventured too close to the bacon slicer and lost a couple of fingers, but the stories always originated with someone who knew someone who knew someone else. There was rarely any evidence of such accidents actually happening, although grocers were sometimes seen with a small, discreet bandage wound around a finger or two.

Greengrocers

Greengrocers' shops were different to grocers' shops; they were more earthy. Where the grocer ran a shop that was pristine, the greengrocer's shop, while not exactly dirty, was definitely redolent of the odour of good, honest dirt on raw vegetables. No one ventured inside without a couple of big, tough, cloth shopping bags. All the vegetables were bought by the pound and tipped straight into the bags, everything on top of everything else: potatoes, carrots, tomatoes, a cucumber, a swede, a cabbage, a cauliflower. All the while the greengrocer, like the grocer next door, would be adding up the cost in his head to deliver a final total price – and only the mathematically adept were in a position to argue – when both bags were full and close to being too heavy to drag out of the shop.

A typical greengrocer's shop of the 1950s.

Confectioners and tobacconists

Imagine a shop window full of shelves, each shelf full of glass jars and each glass jar full to the brim with colourful sweets. That was the sight that enticed customers – especially children – into a 1950s confectioner, more popularly known as a sweet shop. Inside, more jars stood on wooden shelves all around the shop: chocolate limes, pear drops, wine gums, sugar babies, orange creams, coffee creams, mint creams, humbugs, bullseyes, pineapple chunks, all sold by the quarter pound. For children with meagre pocket money there were penny chews, individually wrapped in different flavours; gob-stoppers, large hard balls that did in fact fill the average child-size mouth and which changed colour as they were sucked; liquorice dabs, tubes of sherbet into which a stick of well-sucked liquorice was dipped; flying saucers, made from strange, edible paper, shaped like alien flying machines and also full of sherbet.

Like the grocer, the sweet shop owner would weigh and bag everything with that wrist-twisting, bag-sealing talent that so many food-selling shop owners seemed to possess. Sometimes the proprietors of good sweet shops, in opposition to the growing band of ice cream brands like Wall's

When sweets were sold by the quarter pound from jars.

and Lyons, were also master ice cream makers. Stories were told of sweet shop owners who owned secret recipes known only to themselves and their wives, who in summer sold it in cones and wafers and tubs from a push-up window at the front of the shop that opened directly onto the street. Regular customers would flock from miles around to buy the ice cream because of its special flavour. Rumour had it that baby milk powder was part of the secret of the flavour, but the sweet shop ice cream maker never revealed his secrets and took the recipe to his grave.

Confectioners, however, rarely sold just sweets. They were more often tobacconists too, which meant they sold everything for the smoker from cigarettes to cigars, as well as tobacco for pipes. These were days long before smoking had become an anti-social habit. Indeed, smoking a cigarette was deemed to be the height of sophistication, particularly if you were seen smoking the right make. Craven 'A', for example, advertised its cigarettes by explaining how its smokers remembered 'the cool, firm feel of the natural cork tip, so kind to their lips and recalling the rare flavour of the rich tobacco, so kind to their throats'. Some manufacturers stated that smoking their cigarettes was good for you, and brands fought it out to claim whose product was the healthiest, while the makers of State

Cigarette advertisements from the days when smoking was deemed to be the height of sophistication.

Express 555 cigarettes (British despite their American-type name) were proud to tell everyone that their cigarettes were made under appointment to His Majesty King George VI.

Fishmongers

Some fishmongers ran traditional shops. Others were designed with a counter at the back and, in front of it, a long, flat marble slab that stretched down through the shop and out onto the street. It would be full of all types of fish, lying with their dead eyes open and oblivious to the flies that were dividing their time between here and the chunks of raw meat hanging outside the butcher's shop next door. On a table to one side of the fishmonger's marble slab there might be trays of live eels, slithering and sliding over each other. If a customer wanted to buy one or two, the fishmonger would take them live from the tray, chop them up and wrap them to take away. In the evening, the marble slab would be cleared of any fish not sold during the day but the shop didn't close. From the counter at the back, fish and chips were sold, fresh from huge shiny metal deep-fat fryers. The food was wrapped first in white greaseproof paper and then in newspaper. The paper went soggy when salt and vinegar were applied, and the food always tasted vaguely of newsprint.

Dairy food shops

Dairy products, soon to be absorbed into the general stock of other shops, were once more likely to be sold exclusively in one shop, and at the top of the dairy shop tree stood Sainsbury's. The company was founded in 1869 and its first store opened to sell dairy products in London's Drury Lane in 1904. In 1973, Sainsbury's went public and began opening supermarket-styled stores. But back in the 1950s, the name was represented by large shops, still reflecting those early times to primarily sell butter, eggs, milk, cheese and other dairy products.

Buying butter in Sainsbury's was especially entertaining. Behind the counter, the shop assistants – usually women, rarely men – invited customers to choose what kind of butter they wanted from huge blocks of different types. Once a choice and had been made, along with how much was required, the assistant, a large wooden paddle in each hand, would slice off the right amount, drop it onto a board and then use the paddles to pat it into a cube, flat on all sides, before weighing it and wrapping it in greaseproof paper to take away.

Men's shops

There were certain shops in a 1950s high street into which women rarely ventured. Men's hat shops were among them, and Dunn's was a popular name. They sold nothing but men's hats: trilbies, bowlers, fedoras, panamas, flat caps, newsboy caps, Ascot caps, boaters, pork pie hats, top hats. The shop window was full of them perched on dummy heads. Likewise, Freeman, Hardy & Willis were known for their variety of men's shoes.

Tailors of the time were similarly male dominated. The best known was Montague Burton, named after its founder who opened his first shop, age 18, in Chesterfield with the aim of producing reasonably priced suits for all. 'A five-guinea suit for fifty-five shillings' was his promise.

By the 1950s, with branches in many major towns, the shops were renowned for the excellence of their tailoring and, quite possibly, for introducing a new expression into the English language. One interpretation of the expression 'the full monty', meaning to have the most or the best possible, is that it originated at a time when men went out dressed in the full Montague Burton suit, comprising trousers, jacket and waistcoat.

Burton shop windows displayed a few immaculately dressed tailors' dummies. Inside there were few signs of suits or other clothing, just a shop floor with a large table in the centre on which might be found samples of cloth. The walls of the shop were panelled with wood and full-length mirrors.

Freeman Hardy & Willis were known for their men's shoes.

The male shop assistants were all of a certain age, impeccably dressed, with tape measures hanging around their necks. This was not the place to look for women shop assistants or, indeed, for off-the-peg clothing. Here you would be carefully measured before examining and choosing styles of suit and samples of cloth. You wouldn't be walking out of the shop with a new suit the same day. It would be several weeks before it had been made to measure and ready for collection.

The wonder of Woolworths

Walk down any major high street in the 1950s and eventually you would come to a Woolworths. At least that was what people called it then (the nickname Woolies didn't catch on for many more years.) In fact, gold lettering on a bright red background above the doors of every shop indicated that the real name of the establishment was F.W. Woolworth & Co. Ltd. There was something about Woolworths that was, to most of its customers, quintessentially British. In fact, it was American.

Frank Winfield Woolworth opened his first store in New York in 1879 as a fixed price establishment that initially sold everything for five cents. Later, the cost rose to five and ten cents. Such was the success of the store that its founder was able to have the world's tallest building erected and to pay for it in cash. Stores would eventually be opened all around the world, but the first store outside North America was opened in Liverpool, where goods were sold for either threepence or sixpence. By the 1950s, the fixed price idea had been dropped, but the variety of goods on sale was sustained. It was a department store for every need and type of customer. London might have had Selfridges and Harrods, but it seemed as though every large British town had a branch of Woolworths. And the store sold everything mostly at prices far cheaper than customers could get elsewhere.

The counters were made of wood and sloped from where the shop assistant stood down to where a slender sheet of glass prevented the goods from sliding off onto the floor. Children were encouraged not to hang onto the glass, a particularly difficult instruction to obey around the toy counter. After the toy counter, the electric counter was especially attractive to small boys, where torches with their batteries and bulbs

The manager (centre front) and his staff outside the Woolworth store in Pontypool at Easter 1951.

Christmas displays at Pontypool Woolworth in 1959.

could be bought. If a customer bought a domestic light bulb here, the man behind the counter – the electric department was a place for male shop assistants, rarely female – took it and placed it into one of several different sizes and types of socket arranged on the top of a large wooden box before pressing a switch on the side to light it up. No one bought a light bulb in Woolworths without it being tested first.

Woolworths stores were not brightly lit in the way department stores later became. At the start of the 1950s, light came from incandescent bulbs like bigger versions of household bulbs, in fittings that hung from the ceiling in large, inverted bowl-shaped glass shades. About the second or third week in December every year, the perimeters of the shades were hung with long lengths of silver tinsel, a sure sign that Christmas wasn't far off. By 1959, this old-style lighting had been replaced by fluorescent lighting during modernisation of the stores that took place around the country at this time.

During the early years of the decade, Woolworths banned prams from being brought into the store on Fridays and Saturdays (the store was obviously closed for business on Sundays). Parents who brought children with them on these two days were encouraged to leave their prams under awnings on the doorsteps to take the air while their parents were inside shopping. Although the rule was dropped during the 1950s, it was many

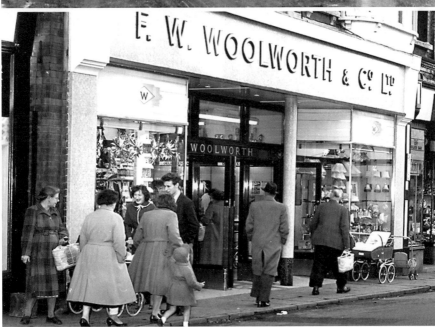

How Woolworths was modernised during the 1950s. Top: The Pontypool store in autumn 1958. Below: The same store after modernisation in May 1959. Note that even then, prams were still left outside.

years before adults could bring themselves to take prams into the store, preferring to carry or walk their children around inside.

During the 1950s, Woolworths introduced food islands to many of its larger stores. Goods were displayed between glass partitions on the counters and customers were also offered special prices on certain products. In 1951, in one of the company's largest branches at The Strand in London, a self-service system was introduced, where customers could help themselves to food off the shelves, take it to a checkout till and leave the store much faster than before. The scheme seemed alien to many customers, but proved popular with busy city workers. The idea pre-empted the arrival of the food-based supermarket that would become popular later the in the decade.

Marks & Spencer

Similar to Woolworths in the way it set out the store, but different in the items it sold, Marks & Spencer was the other big retailer found in most British towns of the 1950s. Just as Woolworth became known as Woolworths, so Marks & Spencer was familiarly referred to as Marks & Spencers or, taking pluralism a step too far, Marks's. The company was founded by Michael Marks in 1884 as a stall in a Leeds open market, selling household goods, haberdashery, toys and sheet music. He called the stall Marks Penny Bazaar, with a sign reading, 'Don't ask the price – it's a penny'. In 1894, Thomas Spencer became a business partner and together they began transforming market stalls into indoor shops. In 1926, the company sold its first bra, and the rest is history. By the 1950s, Marks & Spencer was best known for selling reasonably priced clothing, but was most particularly famous for being the place to which every woman turned for her underwear.

The Co-Op

One other big chain store often found on a 1950s high street was the Co-Op. The company started life in Rochdale in 1844, as a co-operative movement designed to treat all people with respect and to provide affordable food for all. One of its specialities was haberdashery. Some of the lager branches also ran an unusual approach to collecting customers' cash. They were places where, in the words of Dylan Thomas, whose play for voices *Under Milk Wood* debuted on BBC radio in 1954, 'the change hums on wires'. Thomas was describing the interior of an imaginary draper's emporium. In some Co-Op branches of the 1950s the change on humming wires referred more accurately to the rapid wire cash railway system, used in department stores to transport cash from sales assistants to the cashier.

A complicated arrangement of overhead wires ran from all the counters, along which travelled small wooden cups with screw-on bases. The sales assistant unscrewed the base, placed the customer's money into one of the cups, screwed it shut again and pulled a handle, causing the cash to be catapulted along the wire to the cashier, sitting in a small cage in the centre of the store. The cashier removed the money, placed any change that was needed plus a receipt into the cage, then pulled another handle which sent it whizzing back

The pulley and change carrier of a rapid wire cash railway system that was operating at a department store in Hertfordshire during the 1950s and right up until the mid-1980s.

to the sales assistant. Watching the money hum, hiss, buzz and rattle around the store on the wires provided endless amusement for children who might otherwise have been bored stiff waiting while their mothers spent so much time choosing what they needed to buy from an endless assortment of cottons and cloth.

The coming of the supermarkets

With the arrival of supermarkets, the 1950s saw a rise in the popularity of a completely new way of shopping. Until the first supermarket opened, the accepted way was to walk into a shop, go to a counter, ask for what you wanted and wait while the shop assistant found it and handed it to you; and woe betide anyone who touched the merchandise before the handover. With the opening of the first supermarket, shoppers could walk into a store full of shelves displaying an enormous variety of goods, take a basket and help themselves before heading for a checkout point to pay for it all. Many customers admitted feeling a little guilty about taking

Helping themselves to food off the shelf at first seemed alien to 1950s supermarket shoppers.

goods off a shelf before they had been paid for, but the feeing soon wore off, especially when they found the goods were cheaper than in their corner shop.

The idea for a supermarket originated in America and dated back as far as 1916. The concept originally found its way to Britain in 1942 when the London Cooperative Society opened a new type of self-service shop at Manor Park, then a part of Essex, but now a district of East London. Even though food was still on ration, the self-service idea was a success and gradually, the company opened or changed existing branches around the country. Before long, other retailers began to take notice and to follow a similar path.

Express Dairies, who had previously specialised in the home delivery of milk and other dairy products, opened the Premiere Supermarket in London's Streatham High Road in 1951. This was the first time the word supermarket had been used in Britain. Aimed squarely at women, it offered a self-service store where shoppers could purchase rationed and other grocery goods, greengrocery, dairy products, cosmetics, light bulbs, greetings cards and more, all in one surprisingly large shop, and it soon became obvious that a whole week's shopping could be bought in a single visit – a concept that was alien to food shoppers until then. On the first day, about 1,500 shoppers passed through Premiere's doors. While the average British shop at that time took about £98 a week, the new supermarket was soon taking more like £1,000 a week. Throughout the 1950s and into the mid-1960s, Premiere opened another thirty-nine stores around Britain, and became pioneers of the supermarket giants we know today.

Supermarkets didn't just change the way people shopped; they also changed the way food was packaged. Previously, the shopper who wanted biscuits, for example, visited a local store where the biscuits were kept in tins, before being weighed and handed over in bags. With the advent of self-service, biscuits needed to be prepacked in different amounts, ready to be plucked off the shelves, and it was the same with so many other goods that had never before been pre-packed for sale, heralding yet another new way of shopping.

At first, there were those who opposed the idea of supermarkets, seeing them as anti-social compared to the relationship many had with their local shops. Most, however, embraced the new ways. The 1950s by no means marked the end of the small, friendly shopkeeper. But supermarkets brought a major change to the way people shopped and for many of the small shops that lined each side of a 1950s high street, the writing was most definitely on the wall.

Chapter 8

What's on the Wireless?

*Types of radio – domination of the BBC – Radio Luxembourg –
comedy – drama – music – variety shows – detective shows –
science fiction – children's programmes*

FACT BOX

- Radio was the principal source of evening entertainment at the start of the 1950s.
- Valve radios were large and became very hot very quickly.
- Radios needed aerials and earth wires to work correctly.
- The BBC was the world's first public broadcasting service.
- One of the most popular radio shows featured a ventriloquist and his dummy.
- *The Archers* was first broadcast in 1950 and has become the world's longest-running drama series.
- The BBC once transmitted nightly SOS calls to help listeners find missing persons.
- Television became the dominant entertainment source by the end of the 1950s.

At the start of the 1950s, radio – or the wireless, as many still called it – was the principal source of entertainment in the majority of households. Television didn't begin to become popular until 1953, when the coronation of Queen Elizabeth II prompted many to buy or rent their first sets. Even then, and for many years after, radio remained the favourite for household entertainment. It might not have offered moving pictures, but it did provide a vast range of programmes and, unlike television which until 1955 broadcast only one channel, all this was available on a variety of channels – or stations, as they were more commonly known – broadcast primarily in Britain but also emanating from broadcasters overseas.

Radios of the 1950s

Radio receivers, regularly in use no more than a generation before the start of the 1950s, didn't need power. They relied on an electronic component called a crystal detector, together with two other components, normally a coil of wire and a capacitor for tuning, which when wired together

Typical radios of the 1950s, made by Rolland (above) and Phillips (below).

in a specific way picked up a radio signal. The receivers were known as crystal sets and the sound was so weak that it could only be heard using earphones. By the 1950s, radio had progressed to the point where much more complicated circuitry, the use of different types of valves and power from either mains electricity or batteries, was enough to operate a loudspeaker.

Most radios at the start of the decade were large, many made of wood and some from Bakelite. Whatever the material used for the bodywork or cabinet, the various components, most notably the valves, grew hot when in use, and so the cabinets also heated up. In

Small radio, 1950s-style: a Vidor My Lady Margaret 429 portable.

fact, radio sets didn't actually start working until everything was at the right temperature. Once turned on, the listener had to wait a suitable time for the set to 'warm up', and a hot radio gave off a distinctive smell. Their controls usually comprised an on/off knob combined with a volume control, a knob to adjust the base sound and another to adjust the treble, or sometimes one knob to adjust both. A tuning knob was usually coupled to a needle that rotated around a dial or swept across and behind a glass or plastic plate marked with the names of radio stations which the set was reputed to be able to pick up. Stations broadcast by the BBC were the easiest to tune into, but many sets had a wealth of foreign stations marked from which a signal could be received, some weak, others stronger, depending on the time of day or weather conditions. They included Monte Carlo, Paris, Luxembourg, Hilversum, Brussels, Lille, Berlin, Rome, Stuttgart, Oslo and more.

Any radio of this time needed an aerial, which might have been little more than a length of wire attached to a terminal on the back of the set and strung across the room. Many also had an earth terminal to which a wire would be attached with the other end secured to a piece of metal pushed into the soil of the garden outside. It might also be attached to a nearby tap or water pipe that ran into the ground.

Some homes in the 1950s were still not equipped with electricity, relying on gas for lighting. If the radio – and inevitably there would be only one radio to a family – was used in a gas-only house, then it would need a battery, or sometimes several batteries, to power it. These were likely to have been one enormous dry battery and a separate type of wet battery called an accumulator, which comprised terminals inserted into a glass jar of liquid that had to be recharged on a weekly basis.

Those who didn't want, or couldn't afford, to buy a radio often rented one. Companies like Radio Rentals would set up a base in one of a town's shops where they built huge radio receivers. These supplied reception to loudspeakers in the homes of their customers. Each loudspeaker was equipped with an on/off switch combined with a volume control and another knob to change the stations, restricted to those from the BBC. They were connected to the central hub by way of wires from the room containing the loudspeaker up to the roof of the house and from there by wires, like telephone cables, strung across roads and streets and back to the shop that housed the receivers. Rented sets like these were particularly popular with home owners whose houses didn't have electricity. Later, Radio Rentals and similar companies went on to rent out televisions.

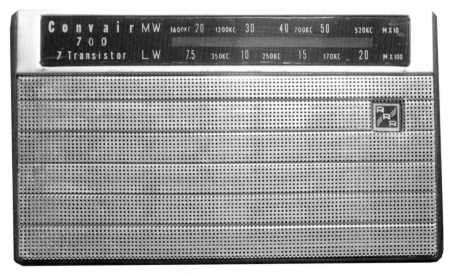

Transistor technology made radios like this seven-transistor Convair 700 model small enough to slip into a large pocket.

With the advent of transistors, radios became smaller, lighter and less prone to giving their owners a nasty burn. The discovery of transistors in 1939 led to a solid state alternative to valves. They were first used in an American radio in 1952, but it was 1956 before the Pye company produced the first British transistor radio. By the end of the decade just about every radio manufacturer had made the leap from valves to transistors, changing for ever the shape, design, affordability, practicality and portability of radios.

BBC radio

The British Broadcasting Corporation, universally known as the BBC, was the world's first public broadcasting service, beginning in London in 1922. Over the years, as more transmitters were opened around the UK, the service expanded, with different programmes for different regions of the country. Then came the Second World War, when problems were encountered with enemy bombers using British radio transmitters for navigation, causing certain transmitters having to be closed down during air raids. Within weeks of the war ending, BBC transmissions were up and running again and, by the start of the 1950s, three familiar stations were available to BBC listeners. The Light Programme broadcast most of the light entertainment content. The Home Service was divided into seven regions that broadcast localised programmes of a more serious nature. The Third Programme, whose broadcasts went out only between 8 pm and 11 pm in the evenings, was mainly for classical music and the occasional serious talk.

Without going too much into the technicalities of radio broadcasting, it is sufficient to know that BBC radio programmes in the early years of the 1950s were broadcast by what is known as amplitude modulation, more commonly referred to as AM. One problem with AM was that some areas of the country couldn't receive the broadcasts with the quality enjoyed by others. Another problem was that foreign radio stations, which also used AM, were on the increase and their broadcasts were likely to interfere with BBC transmissions in the UK. A third problem was that as televisions became more popular it was apparent that their sound quality was better than that from radios. To overcome these problems the BBC invested in a new higher frequency radio transmission system that allowed

Broadcasting House at the end of London's Regent Street, from where so many BBC radio programmes were broadcast in the 1950s.

RADIO LUXEMBOURG

Among the many foreign radio stations that adorned the tuning dials of 1950s radios, one was often more prominent than others. Radio Luxembourg began in 1924 when two brothers, François and Marcel Anen, enthralled by the prospect of radio communication, installed a transmitter in the attic of their house in Luxembourg City. In the years that followed, they set about broadcasting music and sports reports, gradually increasing the power of their transmitters. The station was initially multi-lingual, but in 1933, an English language service began and, by the 1950s, it was possible to receive the station in Britain. It became known as *The Station of the Stars* and was one of the few sources of pop music available to radio listeners who were content to listen to the station's weak signal that continually faded and needed to be retuned.

Radio Luxembourg exhibiting in 1958 at Expo 58, the first major World's Fair after the Second World War.

Not every programme broadcast by Radio Luxembourg originated overseas. Some of its programming began in Britain, but because of the BBC's monopoly it could only be legally broadcast from outside the country. A prime example is a British programme of the 1950s called *The Adventures of Dan Dare*. The hero was a space explorer who originated in the *Eagle* comic where he came up against, and battled, numerous aliens. The programme was produced at a studio in London by John Glyn-Jones, who later won fame as a British television and film actor. Each episode was recorded onto wax discs, which were shipped to Luxembourg for transmission back to Britain. The voice that announced the start of each episode would have been familiar to many a UK listener. He was Bob Danvers-Walker, a radio and newsreel announcer, best known as the voice behind *Pathé News*, which was shown in British cinemas.

Since the BBC was a public broadcasting corporation, paid for by compulsory radio licences, there was never any need for sponsorship or advertising. Not so Radio Luxembourg, whose listeners were initially surprised by the inclusion of advertisements for everything from soap powder to systems for winning the football pools. *Dan Dare* was sponsored by Horlicks, a nutritional malt milk drink, traditionally drunk warm at night before bedtime.

the broadcasting of the Light Programme, Home Service and the Third Programme using a system called frequency modulation, better known as FM. The BBC opened its first FM radio station in 1955, broadcasting to London and the south-east of England. Soon, other transmitting stations were opened and, by the end of the decade, FM broadcasts covered the UK. The first stereo broadcasts, mainly of classical music on the Third Programme, were piloted in 1958.

The programmes

So what of the programmes broadcast by the BBC during the 1950s? They were many and extremely varied, catering for all tastes and all classes of listeners. Programmes included news, music, drama, variety, comedy, serials, documentaries, panel shows, discussions, arts programmes, women's interest, children's programmes, shipping forecasts and even SOS announcements to locate missing or otherwise hard to locate people and bring them important personal news.

Strangely, one of the most popular programmes on 1950s radio fell into none of these categories. It was called *Have a Go*, and it was presided over by Yorkshire actor Wilfred Pickles, who suggested the title. The show was totally unscripted and consisted of Pickles with his wife Mabel touring church halls all over Britain to interview ordinary people from each locality who were encouraged to tell stories about themselves and maybe something of the old times in the area. After that, they were invited to take part in a simple general knowledge quiz to win cash and local products. The cash, which was always won

Actor Wilfred Pickles, the man behind one of the BBC's most successful radio shows of the 1950s.

due to the simplicity of the questions, or prompting from Pickles if the contestant was floundering, totalled £1 18*s* 6*d*, awarded for each of four questions in instalments of half a crown, five shillings, ten shillings and a guinea. When they won, Pickles would utter his catchphrase, 'Give 'em the money, Barney,' referring to producer Barney Colehan, who would be presiding over the table of cash and produce. When Colehan left, his place at the table was taken by Pickles's wife and the catchphrase became, 'Give 'em the money, Mabel.' If the contestant was a young person, or sometimes a really old one, Pickles would produce his other popular catchphrase, 'Are you courting?' *Have A Go* was broadcast from 1946 to 1967, but it was during the 1950s that it reached its peak, attracting audiences of 20 million.

The following is by no means a comprehensive list of all BBC radio programmes of the decade (they could fill an entire book on their own), but it will hopefully give a taste of the variety of interests for which radio catered all day and every day.

Comedy

Of all the many different types of programme broadcast by the BBC, comedy was among the most popular and prolific. It was the place where many well-known comedians and actors cut their teeth before branching out into television and, for some, even to international cinema fame. Who would have thought, for example, that Julie Andrews, most famous for her part in *The Sound of Music*, was once a regular member of the cast of the radio programme *Educating Archie*? Here are some of the radio comedy programmes fondly remembered from the 1950s.

Educating Archie

Of all the ideas for a radio comedy programme, one starring a ventriloquist and his dummy must have been one of the strangest. Yet that was the premise behind *Educating Archie*, first broadcast in June 1950. The ventriloquist was Peter Brough, who began his career at the age of 16 in his family's clothing business, a fact that might have led to him always being dapper and well dressed when he made personal appearances with his dummy Archie, who was dressed in a striped blazer. It was never clear exactly what their relationship was meant to be, although he seemed to be some kind of mentor. Archie always referred to him as Brough, with a disdain that suggested he was the master and Brough was a servant. The dummy, even though the radio audience couldn't see him, sounded like a real but rather naughty schoolboy who continually exasperated Brough.

The show was only meant to run for a few episodes, but soon became so popular that it averaged 15 million listeners for each episode when it was broadcast on the BBC Light Programme. Over the course of many series, Archie had a succession of tutors played

Proving ventriloquism could work on radio: Peter Brough and Archie Andrews.

One of Archie's earliest tutors, Robert Moreton, with what he called his 'bumper fun book'.

by actors and comedians that included Robert Moreton, Tony Hancock, Max Bygraves, Harry Secombe, Bruce Forsyth, Hattie Jacques, Benny Hill and Dick Emery. Beryl Reid played his equally naughty friend Monica, and Julie Andrews, who wasn't more than 16 years old in the early 1950s when the show was first broadcast, played his girlfriend.

Although ventriloquism might seem an odd subject for radio, it proved to be ideal for Peter Brough and Archie Andrews who, when the show transferred to television in 1956, failed to command a big enough audience. When the shows were finally taken off air in 1960, Peter Brough returned to his family's clothing business.

Max Bygraves, who went on to greater fame after being another of Archie's tutors.

The Goon Show

The surreal, unexpected and often daft comedy that became the vogue on television of the late 1960s with the advent of *Monty Python's Flying Circus* was pre-empted nearly twenty years before on radio with the arrival of *The Goon Show*, first broadcast in May 1951. Until then much of radio comedy had followed a fairly predictable format of comedy sketches with musical interludes, and, at the start, *The Goon Show* followed those principles. After a few series, however, the show developed into half-hour episodes each of which told a complete story, interrupted a couple of times by

The Goons, from the top: Harry Secombe, Peter Sellers and Spike Milligan.

music. What made *The Goon Show* so different from any other radio comedy programme was its storylines, which often wandered off into strange flights of fantasy. At first the BBC didn't know what to make of it. Veteran radio producer Charles Chilton, responsible for producing many of the episodes, once told of how the BBC officials even got the name of the show wrong at the start, thinking it was actually called *The Go On Show*.

The initial stars were Peter Sellers, Spike Milligan, Harry Secombe and Michael Bentine, although Bentine soon dropped out. Between them, the three remaining stars played a multitude of characters that included Neddy Seagoon, Major Dennis Bloodnok, Bluebottle, Eccles, Hercules Grytpype-Thynne, Count Jim Moriarty, Henry Crun and Minnie Bannister. Each had their own catchphrase which audiences expected to hear week after week. The shows were written by Spike Milligan and reputedly led to his nervous breakdown in 1952, when other scriptwriters including Eric Sykes helped out and sometimes wrote entire episodes.

The storylines were absurd, bizarre, strange, crazy and sometimes undeniably stupid. Yet underlying them all there was a strange sense of warped logic. The regular characters that populated the stories were caricatures, greatly exaggerated beyond the way any normal person would behave. Yet there was something in each of them with which listeners could identify. It's almost impossible to summarise one or more of the stories that *The Goon Show* told during its ten-year run, but a little of their flavour can be gleaned from a few of the titles under which some of the shows were broadcast: *Where Does Santa Claus Go in the Summer?*, *Where Do Socks Come From?*, *Through the Sound Barrier in an Airing Cupboard*, *The First Albert Memorial to the Moon*, *Ten Thousand Fathoms Down in a Wardrobe*, *The Collapse of the British Railway Sandwich System*, *The Dreaded Batter-Pudding Hurler of Bexhill-on-Sea*, *The Affair of the Lone Banana* and *The Tale of Men's Shirts*.

Hancock's Half Hour

Tony Hancock was a comedian who achieved some fame appearing on radio shows like *Workers' Playtime* and *Variety Bandbox*, as well as his stint as Archie's tutor in *Educating Archie*. His big break came, however, when he teamed up with comedy writers Ray Galton and Alan Simpson, who had previously written for him when he appeared on a show called *Calling All Forces*. Their writing genius was to take Hancock's real-life persona and

Tony Hancock, pictured in an ABC Television publicity picture during his first television series, and while still recording his radio shows.

turn it into a fictitious character who was, at its heart, a highly exaggerated version of the real man. The radio shows, which were first broadcast in 1954, portrayed Hancock, whose real name was used throughout, as a somewhat down-at-heel comedian and aspiring actor, pompous and pretentious with ideas above his station that inevitably came crashing down.

Throughout the run of the shows he was heard to be living in various places, but ended up in his most famous address at 23 Railway Cuttings, East Cheam. (Cheam is a real place in Surrey, East Cheam is not.) While other comedy shows still followed the old variety format of sketches and songs, and even though *The Goon Show* had begun to tell complete stories in each episode, *Hancock's Half Hour* was much more of what would become popularly known as a situation comedy, or sitcom.

Tony Hancock was supported in the shows by a group of comedy actors. Sid James played a likeable crook who usually found a way to con Hancock in each episode; Bill Kerr played his rather dim-witted lodger; Kenneth Williams, with his range of strange voices, played just about every other character in the show. Later, the team was joined by Hattie Jacques, who played Hancock's secretary, Grizelda Pugh. The shows were a tremendous success and there were stories of pubs standing empty on the nights when *Hancock's Half Hour* was broadcast on the radio.

In 1956, while still recording his radio shows, Hancock made the move to commercial television with a short series called *The Tony Hancock Show*, which followed the old series of sketches format. It was not a great success. But in 1956, he made the move to BBC Television, once again teamed up with Galton and Simpson and very successfully transferred the *Hancock's Half Hour* formula to the small screen. By now he had discarded his earlier associates and only Sid James made the transition alongside him to television. Eventually, Hancock jettisoned Sid James as well and went on to make a successful series simply called *Hancock*, still scripted by his original writers. He also made a successful film called *The Rebel*, again scripted by the pair. It was when he finally discarded Galton and Simpson that his career went into decline. One more film, *The Punch and Judy Man*, failed to attract big audiences, even though it has today developed a cult status. In 1968, Tony Hancock went to Australia to try to revive the old Hancock character for Australian television. But by then, he was beset with insecurity, ill health and alcoholism. He took his own life in June 1968 in his hotel room just six months after his arrival in Australia.

Take It From Here

First broadcast in 1946, *Take It From Here* ran on radio throughout the 1950s until its final broadcast in 1960, and was so popular that it encompassed 328 episodes over thirteen series. The show was written for most of its radio lifetime by Frank Muir and Denis Norden. The cast comprised Jimmy Edwards, Dick Bentley and, initially, Joy Nichols. Since she was both actress and singer, she was replaced in 1953 by singer Alma Cogan.

The first series of *Take It From Here* was set, incongruously since the show was put out by the non-commercial BBC, in a commercial radio station. But with the start of the second series, the show fell into the traditional sketch and music formula of so many other radio shows of the time. Each episode was divided into three acts, interspersed with a musical interlude. The first part was in the form of a topical comedy discussion, followed by music from a close-harmony group called *The Keynotes*. Then came a parody sketch which presented mixed genres such as a performance of Shakespeare as a pantomime, or the weather forecast sung as an opera. The second musical interlude came from Dick Bentley or Joy Nichols initially, and Alma Cogan after 1953. The final section was in the form of a sitcom, and it was here that, starting in 1953, *Take It From Here* presented its most popular series of sketches in the shape of the Glum family.

Jimmy Edwards was Mr Glum, father of Ron Glum, a dim-witted character who managed to do everything wrong and get the wrong idea

The three original cast members from *Take It From Here*, left to right: Jimmy Edwards, Joy Nichols and Dick Bentley.

about anything said to him. June Whitfield played his long-betrothed fiancée Eth. Most episodes would be begin with Eth whining, 'Oooo Ron,' to which Ron would reply, 'Yes Eth?' and then they would be off into some storyline which inevitably led to Ron getting the wrong idea about Eth's intentions and moving in for a kiss just as Mr Glum opened the door to proclaim, 'Hello, hello, hello ...' The only other member of the family was Mrs Glum, referred to only as 'Mother', who was never actually heard, apart from as a series of indistinct mumblings, supplied by Alma Cogan.

In 1959, Frank Muir and Denis Norden made the move to television scriptwriting and were replaced as writers of *Take It From Here* by Barry Took and Eric Merriman. It proved to be the last series. In 1979, *The Glums* made the transition to television. The show ran for six episodes, but never gained the popularity, and indeed the love, the public had shown for the radio versions broadcast as a major part of *Take It From Here*.

Other radio comedy

While the shows mentioned so far cover a broad spectrum of BBC radio comedy of this era, they by no means represent the total output of shows of the 1950s. Other radio comedy broadcast during the decade includes ...

Beyond Our Ken: First broadcast in 1958, the show starred Kenneth Horne who was both a comedian and a businessman who had made a career in the safety glass business. He was supported by characters that performed a series of often risqué sketches. The content became even more risqué when, in 1965, and with the same cast, the show was renamed *Round The Horne*

Life of Bliss: Initially starring David Tomlinson (later of *Mary Poppins* fame) then from the second series onwards, George Cole (later to find fame as Flash Harry in the *St Trinians* films and even later as Arthur Dailey in the TV series *Minder*), the shows ran from 1953 to 1969. They involved awkward, absent-minded and gullible young bachelor David Bliss and the way his misinterpretations of life around him led to regular embarrassing situations. His pet dog Psyche was played by animal impersonator Percy Edwards.

The Lyon family, all of whom took part in the *Life With The Lyons* radio series, left to right: Richard, Bebe, Ben and Barbara.

Life with The Lyons: Ben Lyon and his wife Bebe Daniels were both American film stars, who settled in London during the Second World War while they made a radio programme called *Hi Gang*. After the war, they remained in Britain and began making a new radio series first broadcast in 1950. Called *Life With the Lyons*, it ran until 1961, attracting more than 11 million listeners. The show was recognised as one of the first situation comedies to base its plots on recognisable family life.

Meet the Huggetts: Jack Warner (later to become television's favourite police constable, George Dixon) starred with Kathleen Harrison as down-to-earth Joe and Ethel. Light-hearted scripts showed them raising a family in post-war Britain. The shows were broadcast from 1953 to 1961.

Much Binding in the Marsh: Beginning in 1944 and broadcasting until 1954, Kenneth Horne and Richard Murdoch played the senior staff in a fictional Royal Air Force battalion as they daily battled red tape and wartime inconveniences.

Ray's a Laugh: Popular music hall performer Ted Ray headed up a show which took the traditional form of a domestic comedy with musical

From *Ray's a Laugh*: Ted Ray and Kitty Bluett.

interludes. The show, which also starred Kitty Bluett as Ted's wife, ran from 1949 to 1961 and featured early performances from a young Peter Sellers.

The Clitheroe Kid: Comedian James Robinson Clitheroe, taking advantage of the fact that he never grew more than 4-foot 3-inches tall, regularly played the part of a cheeky schoolboy. The shows involved little Jimmy and his family in the north of England, running from 1957 until as late as 1972.

The Navy Lark: HMS *Troutbridge* was the fictitious ship on which a crew of unlikely and incompetent sailors got themselves into and out of various comedic situations. Leslie Phillips, Jon Pertwee and Ronnie Barker were among the cast of the show, which was broadcast from 1959 until 1976, making it the BBC's longest-running radio show.

Up The Pole: An Arctic trading post was the unlikely location for the show, which starred popular cross-talk double act Jimmy Jewel and Ben Warriss, who were sometimes referred to as a British version of the American Abbott and Costello double act. This now almost forgotten radio show ran from 1947 until 1952.

Jimmy Jewel (right) and Ben Warriss, a popular double act from the now largely forgotten radio show *Up The Pole*.

Drama series and serials

While comedy formed a major part of the BBC's radio output during the 1950s, more serious long-running drama series and serials took up significant portions of airtime too. They ranged from the fairly mundane everyday life of ordinary people to alien worlds in outer space, taking in on the way a special agent recognised as a predecessor of James Bond. The following are just four of the more popular serial and series broadcast during the decade.

Mrs Dale's Diary

To the sound of harp music playing what would become an iconic signature tune, *Mrs Dale's Diary* arrived on the BBC's Light Programme in 1948 to run right through the 1950s until it ended in 1969, by which time it had been renamed *The Dales*. The term 'soap' or 'soap opera' was not used in Britain in those days, but if it were, this would have qualified as the BBC's first post-war soap. It concerned Mary Dale, who kept a diary about her daily life; her husband Jim, who was a doctor; and their two children, Gwen and Bob. Other characters included Mrs Freeman, Mary's mother, always referred to by Jim as 'mother-in-law'; and Mary's sister Sally, who was rather posh and lived in Chelsea. Mrs Dale was played by actress Ellis Powell right through the 1950s and was replaced by Jessie Matthews in 1963.

The Dales lived in the fictional London suburb of Parkwood Hill, and they were the epitome of middle-class Britain in the 1950s. The women in the series tended to speak with what some referred to as 'BBC English', in which every 'a' sound became an 'e' sound. Hence, the Dale's cat called Captain was commonly referred to as 'a ket called Kepton'. The cosy plots of each episode were rarely memorable in the early days, though in later years they became a little more controversial. Mrs Dale became a local councillor and had to retire when her careless driving caused a man's death; Jim had to retire from his doctor's practice when he had a heart attack; and Sally's husband eventually came out as gay, a dangerous plot line for a popular series at that time in England.

Whether she actually said it or not, it was popularly reported that most episodes began with Mrs Dale, writing in her diary, 'I've been rather worried about Jim lately.' It was a phrase that became parodied a great deal, not least in the satirical magazine *Private Eye*, where *Mrs Wilson's Diary* (a reference to Mary Wilson, the wife of the then Prime Minister Harold Wilson) made a regular appearance; and in the radio programme *Round The Horne*, which regularly featured a section called *Mrs Dire's Dreary*.

The series was something of which many made fun, even at the height of its success, but it became a post-war institution for the BBC, pulled in listeners by the thousand and even went on to a new life as a London stage play. The run was short and the play was never revived.

The Archers

There was a time when everyone in Britain must have been able to identify the theme music which nightly introduced the fifteen-minute radio series *The Archers*. Ask anyone how it sounded and you'd be told it went, 'Rum-ty-tum-ty-tum-ty-tum, rum-ty-tum-ty-tum-tum, rum-ty-tum-ty-tum-ty-tum-ty-tum-ty-tiddly-tum.' Everyone knew it, but few knew its name. It was actually a piece of music called 'Barwick Green', a maypole dance from a suite called *My Native Heath*, written by Yorkshire composer Arthur Wood in 1924 and said to have been inspired by a view across the Sussex seaside resort of Bognor Regis.

The series began as a week-long pilot first broadcast on 29 May 1950. Introducing each episode, the announcer described it as 'an everyday story of country folk'. Originally produced in collaboration with the Ministry of Agriculture, Fisheries and Food, *The Archers* was seen as a way of keeping farmers and smallholders informed about ways to increase productivity in the post-war years. This meant that it initially attracted a listenership made up mainly of farmers. As the series got into its stride, however, it became more of a drama about all kinds of people who lived in the country. It first aired on the BBC Light Programme at lunchtime, but soon transferred to its regular slot at 6.45 pm every weekday evening.

Dan and Doris Archer were the original patriarch and matriarch who ran Brookfield Farm in the fictional village of Ambridge. They eventually handed the farm down to their son Phil and his wife Jill, and as the series progressed over the years, it fell into the hands of Phil and Jill's four children, David, Shula, Kenton and Elizabeth.

In the early days, one of the favourite characters was an old man named Walter Gabriel, who referred to everyone as 'my old pal, my old beauty' and who spent most of his time pontificating pearls of wisdom in a broad country-yokel type of accent. In 1961, comedian Tony Hancock, in one of his later television shows, brilliantly portrayed a parody of Walter Gabriel with a character called Joshua Merriweather in a spoof of *The Archers* called *The Bowmans*.

The reason why so many Archer generations have been involved in storylines over the years is due to the long life of the series. From its first airing in May 1950, *The Archers* is, at the time of writing (early 2022), still going strong, albeit cut from its original fifteen-minute slot to twelve minutes. More than seventy years after its first broadcast, *The Archers* is the world's longest-running radio serial.

Dick Barton, Special Agent

The Archers was not the only radio series with well-known theme music. To the tune of another piece of music called 'Devil's Galop', Dick Barton made his first appearance on radio in 1946 and only just made it into the 1950s with a series of nightly fifteen-minute episodes. The show aired at 6.45 pm every evening until *The Archers* replaced it in that slot in 1951.

Dick Barton was a kind of early James Bond, an ex-commando who, on a nightly basis, solved crimes, got into incredible scrapes and saved Britain from dastardly villains. Each episode ended with a cliffhanger from which Dick couldn't possibly escape – until he did quite easily at the start of the next episode. His easy escapes from seemingly impossible situations gave rise to the popular catchphrase of the time: 'With one mighty bound, he was free.' The plots, which often verged on the ridiculous but were nevertheless entertaining, had titles that followed a simple formula: *Dick Barton and the … Secret Weapon*, *Cabatolin Diamonds*, *Affair of the Black Panther*, *Li-Chang Adventure*, and many more.

Although Dick Barton's radio fame ended in 1951, he went on to greater things. By that time, three films had already been made by the Hammer company. *Dick Barton: Special Agent*, *Dick Barton Strikes Back* and *Dick Barton at Bay* had been released in 1948, 1949 and 1950 respectively. In 1979, Southern Television resurrected the secret agent in a TV series, and in 1998, a stage musical comedy based on the radio series was premièred at the Warehouse Theatre in South London to great acclaim.

Journey Into Space

Of all the radio serials – as opposed to soap opera types of series – of the 1950s, *Journey Into Space* was perhaps the most popular, and the most ambitious. Broadcast at a time when science fiction films were starting to be popular in the cinema, its weekly episodes kept listeners on the edges of their seats as they journeyed with the crew of various spaceships to the Moon and Mars.

Journey Into Space was written by Charles Chilton, a radio producer who was also involved with other hit radio shows of the 1950s including *The Goon Show* and *The Billy Cotton Band Show*. Although obviously paid for his work as a producer, Chilton was never paid any extra for writing the hit science fiction show. He had no scientific qualifications of his own but was a keen amateur astronomer and was determined that the show's science content should be as accurate as possible. So he enlisted Farnborough rocket designer Kenneth Gatland as technical adviser. Chilton admitted in later years that he wrote the shows from week to week, not really knowing where each episode was going next, usually starting the script on a Friday night, ready for Monday's broadcast.

The cast of *Journey Into Space* around the microphone. Left to right: Don Sharp as Stephen Mitchell or Mitch, Andrew Faulds as Jet Morgan, Alfie Bass as Lemmy Barnet and Guy Kingsley Poynter as Doc Matthews.

The first episode was broadcast on the Light Programme at 7.30 pm in September 1953, but after three weeks the BBC wanted to take it off. Chilton persuaded his bosses that it should be given a chance to run for at least eight weeks. In the end it ran for eighteen weeks, and spawned two more series.

The cast consisted of four main characters. Andrew Faulds, who became a Labour Member of Parliament in 1966, played Captain Jet Morgan. His crew of three were Stephen Mitchell, known at Mitch and played by Don Sharp; Doc Matthews, played by Guy Kingsley Poynter; and Lemmy Barnet, played by David Kossoff in the first series and superseded during the second and third series by Alfie Bass. Slightly ethereal and specially composed music – a rarity in radio drama in those days – was written by Van Phillips, and contributed to much of the production's atmosphere.

In the first 1953 series, subtitled *Operation Luna,* the crew went to the Moon, found life there and travelled through time. The second series, which aired in September 1954, was subtitled *The Red Planet.* In it, Jet and his crew led a fleet of spaceships on a journey to Mars and discovered a Martian plot to invade Earth. It ran for twenty episodes. The third series, which also ran for twenty episodes the following year, was subtitled *The World in Peril*. It saw the crew of intrepid space travellers returning to Mars on a vital mission to obtain the Martian plan for the invasion of Earth, only to find themselves part of the invasion fleet.

Seventeen countries bought *Journey Into Space*. It was translated into half a dozen different languages, from Romanian to Hindustani, and it spawned three books published in 1954, 1956 and 1962. The programme still has a wide fan base today of people who seek out old recordings and collect ephemera connected with the series.

Music lovers, gardeners, children and more

The comedy shows, drama series and serials already mentioned made up a significant aspect of the BBC's radio output. But there were of course many other types of programme regularly broadcast. It would take the rest of this book to list major details of them all, but here is just a flavour of what else was available for daily and nightly listening during the 1950s.

Children's programmes: *Listen with Mother*, each weekday at 1.45 pm, brought music and stories to pre-school age children. Later, at 5 pm, *Children's Hour* was more substantial. By 1950, it had already been on the air for twenty-eight years (originally called *The Children's Hour*) and would carry on broadcasting until 1964. It involved stories, serials and series, several to each episode, which included *Jennings At School*, *Toytown*, *Norman and Henry Bones*, *Sherlock Holmes*, *Worzel Gummidge*, *Winnie-the-Pooh* and an unusual science fiction series called *The Lost Planet*, which dealt with a journey to the planet Hesikos undertaken by an inventor who takes along his schoolboy nephew and cook for company.

Music programmes: *Friday Night Is Music Night*, which began in 1953, presented a programme of light classical, film and theatre music by the BBC Concert Orchestra. True to its title, it was aired on Friday nights. *The Billy Cotton Band Show* was presided over by Billy Cotton, a leader of one of the last big bands, of which there were many more before the Second World War. It comprised a mixture of music, songs and jokes, and ran weekly during Sunday lunchtimes from 1949 until 1968. *Music While You Work*, which broadcast twice daily from 1940 to 1967, played light music, originally aimed at factory workers to be played over factory Tannoy systems. The music content was always happy, upbeat and with a good melody to which workers could sing along or whistle.

Music request shows: The most famous request show was *Family Favourites*, originally devised to unite families in Britain with British Forces serving in West Germany and other places overseas after the Second World War. During its

Billy Cotton, one of the last great big band leaders.

lifetime, it had several presenters, the most famous of which were husband and wife team Cliff Michelmore in Britain, linked with Jean Metcalfe in Germany. The programme was broadcast from 1945 until 1980. *Junior Choice*, broadcast from 1954 to 1982, played music requests for children of all ages, who wrote in to the programme and were thrilled to hear their names mentioned on the radio. *Down Your Way*, broadcast from 1946 to 1992, visited towns and villages all over the country, meeting residents and playing their music requests.

Variety shows: Unlike programmes consisting solely of music, variety shows also included comedy and other novelty acts like animal impersonators. They were places where many soon-to-be-famous comedians cut their teeth. *Workers' Playtime* was one of the best known. It began in 1941 as an effort to boost the morale of industrial workers during the Second World War, but continued as a general variety programme after the war until 1964. Each show was broadcast live three days a week from factory or works canteens, generally referred to as 'somewhere in Britain'. *Variety Bandbox* was another programme that launched the careers of many comedians, including Tony Hancock, Arthur English, Frankie Howerd, Max Wall and Peter Sellers. It ran from 1947 until 1952.

Comedian Arthur English – who always ended his act with the words, 'Play the music, open the cage' – was a regular on *Workers' Playtime* and *Variety Bandbox*.

Even this brief survey of what was being broadcast to Britain every day only truly scratches the surface of the huge amount and diversity of what was on offer. Among the plethora of even more programmes there was *The Nine O'clock News* every night, and *In Town Tonight*, a kind of early form of chat show. There was *Gardener's Question Time* for gardeners; *Merry-Go-Round*, bringing comedy and variety to British troops around the world; panel games like *My Word* and *Does The Team Think?*; conversational programmes like *The Brains Trust*; police shows like *PC 49*; women's interest with *Woman's Hour*; and talks by people that included the poet Dylan Thomas. And there was that same poet's one-off play for voices, *Under Milk Wood*, a milestone of radio broadcasting first heard in 1954, a year after Thomas's death.

It is interesting to note how many programmes launched during, or just prior to, the 1950s were eventually terminated during the mid-1960s, by which time television had taken over as the main source of family entertainment. Radio naturally went on and is still popular today, but the 1950s marked the end of its golden age.

Chapter 9

Watching the Box

*The start of television in Britain – types of television –
one-channel dominance of the BBC – problems of live TV –
the first regular programmes – the arrival
of commercial television*

FACT BOX

- Television was at first available only to people in the south of the country.
- A TV aerial on the roof became a status symbol among some viewers.
- Early televisions could only be watched in a darkened room.
- Television sets were epitomised by very small screens in very large wooden cabinets.
- At the start, the BBC broadcast only thirty hours of TV a week.
- Cars in the street outside interfered with the picture as they passed.
- Programmes stopped at 6 pm every night and recommenced at 7 pm.
- Britain's first television advertisement was for Gibbs SR toothpaste.
- Each night's viewing ended with the National Anthem.

Television wasn't invented in the 1950s; its development originated back in the 1920s. But the 1950s was the decade when television came of age in Britain. In 1950, the number of British homes with a television stood at about 350,000, although transmissions were at first sparse, failing to reach Scotland at all. On 13 February 1952, under the headline 'Scots TV Hope', the *Dundee Courier and Advertiser* reported:

> Television may start in Scotland with the showing of the King's funeral scenes from the Kirk o'Shotts station, which is now almost ready for service. The BBC was unable to commit itself last night, but hoped to comment today on the possibility.

That transmission showing King George VI's funeral was received only across what was known as the Central Belt of Scotland, taking in Edinburgh, Glasgow and immediately surrounding areas. Anywhere further north had to wait another year. In 1953, the coronation of Queen Elizabeth II became a turning point in television ownership throughout the country, with more sales that year, in advance of the coronation broadcast, than in any year previously. After that, the craze for having a box (as many called it) in the corner of the lounge took off fast, and by the end of the decade it was estimated that about three quarters of the UK population owned a television.

This tabletop TV made by Ferguson boasted a 12-inch tube and a neutral colour filter for viewing in strong light.

Viewers more used to relying only on audio entertainment from their radio had to learn a new way of entertaining themselves for a few hours each evening. A small book called *The Television Annual for 1954* revealed the way TV audiences needed to conduct themselves with a whole chapter devoted to what it called 'Fallacies and Facts for Beginner Viewers'. One fallacy it was keen to dispel was the necessity to watch TV in the dark. Early sets, whose small screens were green when turned off, lost all contrast in the picture if a room light was turned on. But by the middle of the decade new screen technology meant that viewing with a table lamp situated behind the set was recommended by the *Annual*, which added, with a nice touch of political incorrectness, 'allowing mother to get on with darning the socks if she wants to'.

Neither was it desirable to have a big screen. Purchasers of moderate priced sets were told to feel in no way inferior to those who lavished money on larger screens. The truth was that most modern drawing rooms needed no more than a 12-inch screen. Anything more than that would reveal the dark lines that made up the picture, meaning viewers would have to sit a long way from the set for the best viewing experience. In many homes, the *Annual* suggested rather condescendingly, that would mean sitting in the hall.

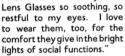

TeleLens television glasses were claimed to be scientifically created to reduce TV glare.

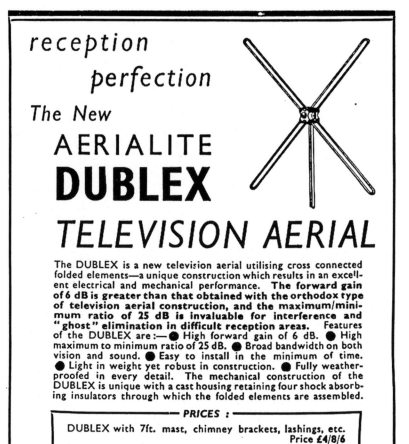
TV aerials were more than a means of receiving broadcasts; many saw them as status symbols as well.

As the popularity of TV increased, it wasn't long before ownership of a set began to be seen as a status symbol, and what better way to boast that you were one of the chosen than to nail an H-shaped aerial to your chimney, even though it wasn't strictly necessary for those who lived close to the transmitter, and who might make do with an indoor aerial, which unfortunately could not be seen by the neighbours.

One surprise that new viewers had to face was that TV programmes were not regionalised. On radio, they could listen to broadcasts from their own regions on the Home Service and, if they didn't like that, they could turn over to the Light Programme for more general entertainment. There

A Radio Rentals leaflet from the 1950s.

An advertisement for Television Mainstal, a company that repaired TVs under contract.

were no such luxuries with television, where one single channel broadcast the same programme to everyone in the country. If anyone complained, the broadcasters had the answer: don't bother to watch. They reckoned it was a good way to counter those stick-in-the-muds who maintained that television ruined the art of conversation or prevented engagement in more creative pursuits.

Not everyone bought their televisions outright or even on hire purchase. It was very common in the 1950s, and for many years after, to rent a set from a company like Radio Rentals, formed in Brighton initially to rent out radios, and who later branched out into renting and selling televisions. The advantages to viewers of renting over buying was the way the rental company built the cost of repairs into the monthly rent, appearing to offer repairs and replacement of parts for free. At a time when it was accepted that television sets would break down at regular intervals and often need expensive tube replacements, many people took the rental route.

Types of TV

The first televisions incorporated a cathode ray tube – the front of which was actually the screen – that was circular in shape but with the picture appearing as a rectangular image in the centre of it. Since this central rectangle was all the viewer needed to look at, the cabinets of these early models were proportionally much larger than the screen, in order to incorporate the part of the tube that viewers didn't need to see. It wasn't uncommon for early TV sets to be as big as a small sideboard, with a

The Aristocrat

of Radio and Television

R·G·D

There's a place for R.G.D. television in your home too !
For these receivers add to the joys of life, both by their
superb appearance and high performance.

Model 2351T has a 12-inch tube and is housed in a figured
walnut cabinet.

Your local R.G.D. Retailer will gladly arrange a demonstration.

ACCREDITED   DEALERS   IN   EVERY   TOWN

Televisions of the 1950s became part of the lounge furniture, as shown in this advertisement for a
British-made RGD model.

screen hardly larger than a goldfish bowl. But as the 1950s progressed, rectangular tubes became more common, with the viewing area covering the whole of the front of the tube, meaning the cabinets that housed the tube could be much more compact.

Even so, televisions were still big. Walnut was the favoured wood for the cabinet, which also often included radios and even gramophones with places to keep records. Some were made to stand on the floor with the screen above a huge loudspeaker and with doors on the front to cover both when viewing was not taking place, making it look more like a 1950s cocktail cabinet. There were those

Some sets had doors that folded across the screen when not in use. This one was fitted with castors for easy movement.

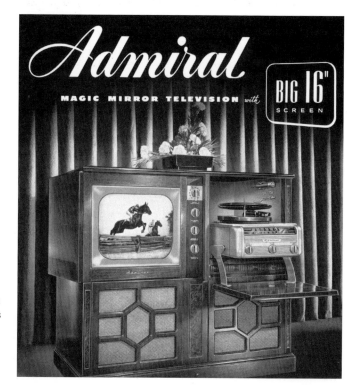

Some TV sets even incorporated radios and gramophones. This one is an American model made by Admiral.

Some TVs acted as projectors, throwing a larger than usual picture onto a screen or even a light-coloured wall.

who considered watching TV somewhat vulgar, so the doors disguised the set when disdainful visitors came calling. As technology improved, televisions became smaller, neater and capable of being placed on a table. Doors across the screen disappeared, but it became popular to have cloth fronts, particularly over the loudspeaker, sometimes with fancy designs to match in with the décor of the room in which the TV was situated.

The sets could be complicated to operate, needing several control knobs to maintain the picture quality throughout the evening's viewing. Volume and the brightness of the screen were the two most important controls and many sets catered for this with just two knobs on the front, the volume knob doubling as an on/off switch. All the other controls were

Controls could be complicated, as demonstrated by this Bush television, seen from the front and back.

either on the side or hidden away at the back. When the set was turned on it initially needed a minute or so to 'warm up', after which the volume and brightness could be adjusted. Contrast of the picture was also an important factor, but that control was likely to be at the back of the set, along with two other important controls known as the horizontal hold and vertical hold. If the picture began to drift sideways, the horizontal hold was employed to bring it back. If the picture flipped up and down, then the vertical hold needed to be adjusted. Since both of these latter two controls were nearly always in the form of very small knobs at the back of the set, the viewer was forced to adopt a difficult stance that involved the contortions of reaching an arm around the back of the set and locating the right knob by feel while trying to crane his or her neck to see the results of such endeavours on the screen at the front.

If a car went by in the street outside, interference in the shape of undulating wavy lines often filled the screen and the contrast had to be readjusted. If the kid next door had a model railway, that too could produce interference on the screen. Even something as simple as switching on or off a light in another room with a badly insulated switch that caused a small internal spark could affect the picture, requiring more adjustments of controls at the front and back of the cabinet. All of which was considered perfectly normal for an evening's viewing. Indeed, many TV owners prided themselves on understanding far more than the simple operation of a few knobs. Witness a letter written to the September 1955 issue of *Practical Television* magazine:

I bought second-hand an HMV television model 1808 AC/DC. Switching on for testing I found no raster, so I decided to connect the aerial to find if the sound section was OK. I then found I had sound, also a picture, but line-hold control was at the end of its travel and would not lock – timebase giving me multiple pictures. I tried all service hints in the September 1954 issue of *Practical Television* – all to no avail, but on insertion of approximately a 10K resister in parallel with the 25K variable horizontal hold, I now have a picture which I can hold. Have you any suggestions?

The remarkable thing is that the editors of the magazine, and quite possibly most of its readers, knew exactly what the correspondent was talking about.

The programmes, of course, were in black and white, although there were those who tried to convince themselves otherwise. On sale in the 1950s were large, square pieces of plastic, coloured green at the bottom, orange in the middle and purple at the top. Viewers put these in front of their black and white sets and kidded themselves they were watching in colour.

The BBC

The British Broadcasting Corporation, or BBC, was solely responsible for the single channel broadcast into the homes of TV viewers of the early 1950s. Formed in 1927, initially under the name of the British Broadcasting Company, the BBC operated under royal charter and was publicly financed by a Post Office licence fee originally of ten shillings, payable by anyone who owned a radio, and later by owners of televisions as well. Its charter right from the start was to entertain and educate by means of broadcast, but very soon the word 'inform' was added so that

The BBC was the only television broadcaster in the first half of the 1950s.

the BBC's mission became to inform, educate and entertain its radio listeners and, later, its TV viewers as well.

The Corporation made its first TV broadcast in 1936, but service was interrupted by the Second World War, which broke out in 1939 and lasted until 1945. After the war, a television service was resumed and, by 1950, the BBC was broadcasting thirty hours of programmes each week. Following the rush to buy televisions for the 1953 coronation, the output had grown to fifty hours a week by 1955.

The number of hours in a day that the BBC was allowed to broadcast was strictly controlled by the Postmaster General, a cabinet-level ministerial position in the Government (a post that was abolished in 1969). At first, the potential to broadcast was allowed only between 9 am and 11 pm, providing no more than two hours were broadcast before 1 pm. Between 6 pm and 7 pm nothing was broadcast at all. This hour became known as the toddlers' truce because it allowed parents to fool their children into thinking TV had finished for the night, in order to get them into bed early. That practice ended in 1957. On Sundays between 2 pm and 4 pm, only programmes of interest to adults were shown because it was assumed children would be in Sunday school. Every evening ended with the playing of the National Anthem.

The perils of live TV

All programmes were broadcast from Alexandra Palace in North London, part of which was leased by the BBC from 1935 expressly for the purpose. Broadcasts began in 1936 and resumed from the same place after the war. Every broadcast was live, transmitted by a 215ft high aerial mast built above the BBC's studios.

Nigel Kneale was a television and film writer who worked on a great many productions for the BBC in the 1950s. He was the writer who created *Quatermass*, in a trio of science fiction serials that scared the public more than any other TV programme ever had and was responsible for the BBC adopting the 'Not Suitable for Children' slogan that prefaced certain programmes thereafter. Interviewed many years later, he recalled some of the perils of live broadcasting:

In 1955, we were broadcasting a play called *The Creature*. It was about the Abominable Snowman. The production was live, and actors were

A scene from *The Quatermass Experiment*, the BBC's first science fiction serial written specifically for television.

in a studio surrounded by scenery meant to look like an ice cave in the Himalayas. About fifteen minutes before the end of the play, the actors, wrapped in the kind of clothes needed when you're supposed to be 20,000 feet up a mountain, looked out of the cave and there, in plain view, was a man in shirtsleeves, sweeping up the snow. It turned out he was a cleaner who wanted to get home early and so had started clearing up the studio while the live broadcast was still going on.

Kneale also wrote the script for BBC Television's adaptation of George Orwell's dystopian novel *Nineteen Eighty-Four*, the broadcasting of which on a Sunday evening caused such a furore with the public that questions were asked in Parliament about its suitability for television audiences. The production also caused a few headaches for the producers during the live broadcast, as Kneale later recalled:

A key element in the plot revolved around a paperweight, found by the hero in an antique shop, and we had a Victorian example to be used in the play. It was left on the prop table, and ten minutes before we went out live, someone stole it. The producer said he was going to black out the studio so that the culprit could return the crucial prop and no questions would be asked. The lights went out. The lights came back on. The prop was still missing. The live performance began, in the knowledge that the paperweight would be needed about halfway through the play. So the stage manager's assistant went home on a bus, borrowed his sister's toy Mickey Mouse snow dome, took a bus back to the studio and got it onto the set in the nick of time.

They were stressful, yet exciting times for all those involved. As Nigel Kneale commented many years later:

> At the end of an evening of broadcasting, I used to walk out onto the top of the hill on which the Alexandra Palace was situated and look down at all the houses below us with television aerials on their roofs, and I'd think to myself how strange it was that people in all those houses have been watching what we have just been doing in that building behind me. It was exhilarating in a way that programme makers today could never feel.

The programmes

Programmes put out by the BBC during the early years of the 1950s were varied but, more often than not, a little staid. Probably the best variety programme was Saturday night's *Café Continental*. As the programme began, a commissionaire walked towards the TV screen, saluted, and gestured as though he were opening the door of the viewer's taxi, before the same viewer was led through a door into the 'club', which was actually a television studio. Such was the fame of this programme that Josephine Baker, famous star of the Folies Bergère, was enticed to appear. For fans of light classics, Eric Robinson presented *Music For You*. For food enthusiasts, there was Philip Harben, star of TV's first cookery show, and famous for his beard and striped apron. For children, there was *Muffin the Mule* and *Peregrine the Penguin*, marionettes who clattered around the top of a piano played by Annette Mills, sister of film actor John Mills. The first TV serial started in those days too. It was called *Little Red Monkey* and involved the killing of British atomic scientists. The little

HOW TO BE AN ANNOUNCER

Between all the live programmes in the 1950s, an announcer appeared on screen to comment on what had gone before and to explain what was coming next. Announcers like Sylvia Peters, Mary Malcolm and McDonald Hobley became household names. Both men and women dressed as though they were attending some high-class function. For the men, the dress code was easy, so long as they wore a suitably serious suit. For women announcers it was different. They were required to dress according to the type of entertainment that was to be broadcast in the evening ahead. In general, women announcers wore evening gowns adapted to be simple or elaborate, according to whether the forthcoming programmes were straightforward or depicting especially grand moments.

In making the announcements between programmes, women in particular needed to present themselves in exactly the right way. It was accepted that a trained actress would have the right experience of speaking to the public. But she had to overcome any tendency to act with a personality that she might imagine fitted in with the programme about to be aired. She was, after all, an announcer, not a character in a forthcoming play. By the same token, she had to guard against being too bland and robot-like in her speech.

Announcers, both men and women, also had to adopt the knack of changing their tone according to the programme that had just finished and the one about to start. As an example, the sequence of programming might mean that something like the annual service of remembrance at the Royal Albert Hall was followed by a variety show. In that circumstance, the announcer would begin by speaking in a fairly sombre tone as he or she mentioned the end of the preceding programme, then gradually move into a more frivolous tone of speech as the following variety show was announced.

At the end of the day, TV audiences had to see the announcers as a cross between a slightly aristocratic person that they wouldn't normally mix with and a family member joining them in their lounges every evening.

red monkey turned out to be a Russian midget who was stealing secret papers, and generally doing dirty deeds.

To get a flavour of what one day's BBC TV entertainment looked like, take a look at Christmas Day 1952, the one day of the year when the broadcaster might be expected to pull out all the stops and give its viewers the cream of the televisual programming crop. For those inclined to sit and watch TV all day, here's what they got:

11.00 am: Christmas Day Service from the Church of St Dunstan and All Saints, Stepney in East London.

12.00: Closedown for the next three hours and twenty minutes.

3.20 pm: *Swiss Miss*, a 1938 film starring popular American comedy double act Laurel and Hardy.

4.20 pm: A ten-minute interlude, in which viewers could watch a short film such as a potter making a pot using a potter's wheel, the sails of a windmill turning in the breeze, someone playing a harp, a bonfire, a field being ploughed, a moonlit landscape … and many more such soothing subjects.

4.30 pm: *For the Very Young*, a programme of Christmas songs and games, with marionettes *Andy Pandy* followed by Bill and Ben in *The Flowerpot Men*.

5.00 pm: Children's Television, presenting a Christmas play called *One Way Genie*.

6.00 pm: Closedown for one and a half hours.

7.30 pm: The highlight of the evening, in the shape of *A Christmas Party* with guests that included Arthur Askey, Ethel Revnell, Norman Wisdom, Frankie Howerd, Petula Clark, Betty Driver, John Slater, Eamonn Andrews, Tommy Cooper and Joe Stuthard, with music by Eric Robinson and his Orchestra. All were top stars of the day.

9.15 pm: Just in case viewers were now feeling too cheerful, *A Christmas Card from Korea* involved a visit to a family in Scotland in which they received greetings from their son serving with the Black Watch during the then current Korean War.

9.30 pm: A musical comedy called *1066 and All That*, based on a popular book, first published in 1930.

11.00 pm: Weather and News – broadcast as sound only, since the curfew for broadcasting TV pictures ended at 11 pm.

11.15 pm: Closedown and the playing of the National Anthem.

It was a night's viewing that fulfilled the BBC's mission of informing, educating and entertaining, even if the content for Christmas Day was a little livelier than most days. After all, the BBC's monopoly of being the only television broadcaster meant it could give its viewers what the Corporation thought they should have, rather than maybe what they actually wanted. If a viewer didn't like what was being presented, then hard luck. There was no alternative. But at 7.15 pm, on 22 September 1955, all that changed.

The arrival of commercial television

At 9.01 pm on 22 September 1955, British television history was made as the country's first TV advertisement was broadcast.

It followed the Television Act of 1954, after which the Independent Television commercial network came into being. For the first time, advertisements were shown before, after and during TV shows. The BBC, in an effort to distract viewers from watching its new rival, might have been expected to broadcast something spectacular on the night of the ITV launch. In fact it did no such thing. Looking somewhat contemptuously down its nose at the new ITV upstart, the BBC chose instead to entice viewers away from watching the launch of ITV by broadcasting something dramatic on the radio! That night, as ITV began its first broadcast, Grace Archer, one of the most popular characters in *The Archers*, the most popular of all the radio drama serials, died in a fire.

A contemporary console TV model for receiving both BBC and ITV. Advertisements for this model added that the set was also 'provided with facilities for the reception of the latest Frequency Modulation Sound radio programmes on the new VHF bands, with freedom from background noise and interference from continental or local sources'.

Meanwhile, ATV, the London arm of ITV, went live with an outside broadcast from the London Guildhall to celebrate the launch of the new channel, with speeches by the Lord Mayor of London and Postmaster

General and the playing of the National Anthem. The evening continued with a variety show starring Harry Secombe and Hughie Green, a performance of Oscar Wilde's play *The Importance of Being Earnest*, and boxing. The very first British TV advertisement to be seen during the evening was for Gibbs SR toothpaste, lasting seventy seconds. Initially, the broadcast could only be seen by viewers in London.

It was a rather staid beginning. But soon, as ITV networks spread around the country, bringing the new commercial channel to more and more people, viewers found themselves watching programmes that were a lot more lively and slick than they had been used to. The pressure from advertisers to get viewers for their advertisements meant the ITV programmes tended towards the populist style of entertainment with soap operas like *Emergency Ward 10*, quiz shows like *Take Your Pick* and a lot more light entertainment in the shape of programmes like *Opportunity Knocks*. ITV also imported American comedy shows like *I Love Lucy* and detective series such as *Dragnet*, the like of which British audiences had never seen before.

At last British television audiences were getting what they wanted, rather than what the broadcaster thought they ought to have. As a result, British audiences deserted the BBC to such an extent that, within the first few years, ITV had taken 70 per cent of the BBC viewers. Clearly, the BBC had to change if it was to survive as a television broadcaster. It did so by adding more popular light entertainments to its schedules, and gradually the viewing figures began to even out.

In order to receive the new commercial channel, viewers had to initially have their television sets converted with a switching arrangement attached to the back, and the electrical magazines were full of articles on how readers could build their own converters. Later, of course, TV sets were manufactured and sold with the new channel option built in. It was another decade before British television audiences could receive a third channel. That was in April 1964, when BBC 2 was launched. A few minutes before the new channel aired, a power cut struck the whole of West London, causing BBC 2 to begin life in almost total darkness and a fair amount of chaos among the broadcasters.

Chapter 10

Going to the Flicks

The popularity of cinema – British film studios – Saturday Morning Pictures – film genres – the arrival of widescreen

FACT BOX

- Many went to the cinema regularly every week irrespective of what was showing.
- With cinemas open all afternoon and evening, people often arrived in the middle of a film, watched it to the end, and then watched it again from the beginning.
- By the start of the 1950s, there were nearly 300 Odeon cinemas in Britain.
- Ealing Studios in West London released about forty films during the 1950s.
- The end of the Second World War led to a glut of war films.
- It wasn't uncommon for stage shows with singers and dancers to be integrated with the film in a cinema.
- *Ben-Hur,* one of the most popular epic films of the 1950s, ran for three hours forty-four minutes, had 365 speaking parts and cost $15 million to make.
- Large cinemas featured organs that were played by an organist during an interval between films.

People didn't go to the cinema in the 1950s; they went to the pictures, or sometimes they went to the flicks. They didn't go to the movies, at least not in Britain. Going to the movies was more of an Americanism. It's easy to see why going to watch moving pictures on a big cinema screen would lead to the expression 'going to the pictures'. The saying 'going to the flicks', however, is a little more obscure. It came about because moving pictures rely on a series of still pictures or frames which, when projected in sequence, thanks to an optical illusion known as persistence of vision, combine in the brain to give the illusion of a

Four cinemas that had been active for many years by the 1950s and which continued in business for many years more. Clockwise from top left: The Electric Palace in Harwich, Essex; The Globe in Worthing, Sussex: The Rio in Burnham-on-Crouch, Essex; and The Palace in Broadstairs, Kent.

single moving image. In the early days of cinema, there was a significant flicker between the frames, hence people spoke of 'going to the flickers'. By the 1950s, the expression had become 'going to the flicks', with few understanding, or really caring, why their favourite weekly pastime was so called.

And it really was a weekly pastime. At the beginning of the decade, with so few homes owning a television, the local cinema was a major source of visual entertainment. Some had a huge cinema organ that emerged from the floor below the screen with the organist playing as he ascended during the interval, only to sink back into the floor again as the evening's main feature film began. Others even had stage shows with

Cinema stars of the 1950s as depicted on cards given away with packets of the London-based company Jibco Tea. Top, left to right: Howard Keel, Kay Kendal, Donald Sinden, Debbie Reynolds and Norman Wisdom. Bottom, left to right: Dirk Bogarde, Jack Hawkins, John Gregson, Jane Powell and Alec Guinness.

singers and dancers who entertained before the film. There was a weekly change of film and many people went every week, irrespective of what was showing. Every town had at least one cinema, many had two and some had even more.

Cinema names

Whether they were part of large chains, or small independent establishments, cinemas of the 1950s rejoiced under names like the Capitol, the Essoldo, the Roxy, the Regal, the Granada, the Palace, the Empire, the Electric, the Globe, the Rio (often referred to by patrons as the R-ten, in reference to the way the name looked in capital letters – R10) and, of course, the Odeon.

By the 1950s, the Odeon cinema chain was the largest in the country, originating with businessman Oscar Deutsch, who opened his first cinema in Birmingham in 1930. By the start of the 1950s, he had close to 300 cinemas operating throughout Britain. The Odeon name dates back to amphitheatres in ancient Greece, and was used in France and Italy in the 1920s before Deutsch appropriated it for his own use, doing little to deny

The Odeon in Burnley, Lancashire, in 1952, when the film being shown was *The Big Trees* starring Kirk Douglas.

Long queues to get into cinemas, like this one for the Empire and Ritz in London's Leicester Square, were a common sight in the 1950s.

the popular misconception that the word had actually been invented as an acronym for 'Oscar Deutsch Entertains Our Nation'. Today's cinemas, often built into shopping malls with frontages little different from the entrances to department stores, are a long way removed from the grandeur of the buildings that were once emblazoned with the Odeon name. Some had originally been run as independent cinemas or parts of smaller chains before being taken over by Deutsch; many were purpose-built. The buildings were large, because they had to house a lot of people; they were high because they utilised a ground floor and at least one, maybe two, balconies above, usually referred to by patrons simply as upstairs and downstairs; and, because cinema entertainment took place in the dark, there were no windows. It made the cinema building itself a somewhat ugly edifice, all the more reason why the entrances should be so lavish.

British film studios

The British film industry – or, to be more precise, the English film industry – was alive and well in the 1950s. Studios active during the decade included Beaconsfield Film Studios, Denham Film Studios and Pinewood Studios in Buckinghamshire; Bray Studios in Berkshire; Bushey Studios and Elstree Studios in Hertfordshire; Shepperton Studios in Surrey; Merton Park Studios and Gainsborough Pictures in London … and many more.

One studio that stood at the heart of the British film industry at this time was Ealing Studios, based in West London. Film-making began on the site as early as 1902, when films were still silent. The sound stages opened in 1931, and films were first released under the Ealing name from 1938. Throughout the 1940s and into the 1950s, Ealing Studios made many serious dramas that became classics. Between 1950 and 1959 alone the studios turned out about forty titles – that's an average of one film every three months. The studios, however, are best remembered for what became known as the Ealing comedies, released at the rate of about one a year. Many of the films adopted a slightly dark and sometimes sinister theme rarely seen in popular comedy films of the time.

Some, though not all, of the Ealing comedy favourites (a few of which were actually made in 1949) that found their way onto the screens of British cinemas in the 1950s included …

Ealing Studios, home to some of the best-loved British comedy films of the 1950s.

Passport to Pimlico (1949): Unearthed treasure and documents indicate that a small area of Central London is actually part of the House of Burgundy, exempt from British rule and requiring those entering the area to have a passport.

Whisky Galore! (1949): What happens when a ship carrying 50,000 cases of whisky is wrecked off a fictional Scottish island, much to the delight of its inhabitants.

Kind Hearts and Coronets (1949): The aggrieved son of a woman disowned by her aristocratic family murders the eight people in line ahead of him to attain his title as a duke.

The Lavender Hill Mob (1951): A humble clerk who has been in charge of gold bullion deliveries for twenty years hatches the perfect plan to steal the gold and retire.

The Man in the White Suit (1951): A young scientist invents an everlasting fibre that never wears out and never gets dirty.

The Titfield Thunderbolt (1953): Villagers attempt to keep a railway branch line open after the Government decrees it should be closed.

Touch and Go (1955): Problems with both family and bureaucrats arise for a man who, unhappy with his life, decides to emigrate to Australia.

The Ladykillers (1955): Perhaps the most famous of the Ealing comedies, concerning a gang of hardened criminals who, following a robbery, hide out in rented rooms owned by an eccentric old lady who unwittingly becomes their accomplice.

Barnacle Bill (1957): The last true Ealing comedy, about a Royal Navy captain trying to live up to family traditions as he manages a run-down seaside amusement pier, part of which inevitably floats away with him on board.

A night at the flicks

Here's how a typical Saturday night out for a 1950s cinemagoing audience might have seemed …

The cinema is a brightly lit oasis in the middle of the dark town, its name emblazoned across the top in neon lighting and the entrance, under a highly illuminated canopy, a symphony of glass doors and bright chrome fittings. Because it's Saturday, the most popular night for going out, there are likely to be more people outside than there are seats inside, so cinemagoers have to queue. Patrons form orderly queues behind signs denoting the available seat prices. There are the one and nines (1s 9d), downstairs close to the screen; the two and sixes (2s 6d, or half a crown), still downstairs but further back where the view of the screen isn't quite so eye-straining; and the three and twos (3s 2d), upstairs for the posh people. On the wall beside the queues, glass-fronted display cases contain collections of photographs called lobby cards that show scenes from the day's main feature film.

The queues are presided over by the commissionaire, a man wearing a peaked cap, white gloves and a long overcoat. No one understands how he knows when the seats inside are full, but at any moment he is likely to hold his arm across one of the queues, often splitting a family in half, to announce that there are no more one and nines tonight. The remainder of the disappointed queue either goes home or reluctantly shuffles over to join the end of the queue for the next price up.

Inside, there is another queue, this time for the glass-fronted ticket booth, in which a woman sits dispensing tickets that shoot out of unexpected slots in the surface of the metal desk over which she presides. There is a different slot for each ticket price. The tickets are half price for children, as is evidenced by a mother with her small son, who asks for 'one and a half, three and twos' before moving off to the staircase that leads to the upstairs. Less rich patrons, who nevertheless see themselves as a cut above the one and nine brigade, go for the two and sixes. That way they'll be downstairs, far enough away from the screen for a comfortable viewing experience but, almost as important, a good way under the balcony above. Consequently, they will escape the tubs of half-eaten ice cream, sweet wrappers, apple cores and the like with which people in the front row of the balcony enjoy showering the audience below. Through the doors that lead to downstairs, people are shown to their seats by an usherette with a torch. The last complete performance is about to start. The last complete performance is so called because this is the last time today that the complete performance will be shown in full from start to finish. In fact, the films have been showing continuously since two o'clock this afternoon. Many people don't bother timing their visit to coincide with the start of a performance. They just turn up when they like, go into the cinema when one of the films is already showing, watch it to the end, then stay through the next performance until they get to the point where they arrived. Watching a major film from the middle to the end, followed a few hours later by watching it again from the start to the middle, was not at all uncommon. If you hear people today saying, 'This is where I came in', that's where the phrase originated. Neither is it unusual for some to arrive for the first performance at two o'clock and stay until the end of the last performance at ten-thirty.

The lights go down and the projector beam from the back comes on, highlighted by cigarette smoke, drifting and curling in the light. The performance begins with the second feature, sometimes referred to as the B-picture, usually a detective story of some kind, shot in black and white and made on a low budget specially to support the main feature. It goes

SATURDAY MORNING PICTURES

While most children of the 1950s went to the cinema along with one or both of their parents, there was one time every week when they were allowed into local cinemas on their own. Saturday Morning Pictures began before the Second World War, closed during the war, then were resurrected after hostilities at the end of the 1940s, and were particularly popular in the 1950s. As its name implies, the performances took place every week on Saturday mornings, when it seemed like the entire younger population of whole

A special ABC Minors Club badge, issued for the coronation in 1953.

towns converged on their local cinemas. At the peak, nearly 2,000 British cinemas put on Saturday morning shows for children.

Most of the major cinema chains had their own clubs for the Saturday morning audiences, the most famous of which was probably the one organised by Associated British Cinemas. Its club was known as the ABC Minors, and members had their own badges. Very wisely, many cinema managers closed the balcony areas and restricted their audiences to sitting downstairs during the performances.

The morning's entertainment followed pretty much the same formula, whatever the cinema chain. It would start with the cinema manager, or one of his staff, coming on stage to welcome everyone. Then there would be the singing of the club song, with different words according to each cinema chain shown on screen with a little bouncing ball jumping across the words to keep everyone in time with the music. Members of the audience might come on stage to partake in competitions, which included quizzes or demonstrations of yo-yo and hula-hoop dexterity, and those who were celebrating their birthdays that morning might be invited up to receive a cheap gift. Then it was on to the morning's films. They usually involved a couple of cartoons, then the main film, which was a lot older than any member of the audience, usually a comedy or something involving cowboys and shoot-outs in places that always seemed to include a lot of rocks. There might also be a weekly serial to encourage the audience to return the following week to find out how a particularly nasty cliffhanger for the hero was resolved. And, of course, there was ice cream.

With weekly entry costing sixpence, another threepence for a bar of chocolate to take in and threepence for an ice cream to buy inside and eat during the performances, most parents considered a shilling to get the kids out of the house and safely entertained on a Saturday morning to be a pretty sound investment.

on for a boring hour and a half. A newsreel follows, often *Pathé News*, a novelty for people who have only a radio at home and so are unfamiliar with seeing the news illustrated by moving pictures. Next come trailers for next week's films, before an interval when all the lights come on and ice creams and drinks are sold by usherettes with trays slung on straps around their necks, walking backwards down the aisles between the rows of seats. In some of the smaller, maybe family-run, cinemas, pots of tea, ordered before the performance began, are passed down the rows. Finally, nearly two hours after first entering the cinema, the lights go down and the main feature begins. When it finishes, as the final credits start to roll up the screen, the audience, as one, makes a dash for the exits to avoid having to stand in awkward silence as the evening's performance ends with the playing of the National Anthem.

All of this was beautifully portrayed in a 1957 film called *The Smallest Show on Earth*, about a young married couple who inherit a ramshackle old cinema. In 1963, American author Ray Bradbury, who had lived in Ireland during the 1950s, wrote a short story called *The Anthem Sprinters*, which told the tale of rebellious cinema audiences who made a sport of getting out of the cinema in the brief moments between the end of the film and the start of the National Anthem.

Film genres of the 1950s

The 1950s saw the release of films that covered every genre, from slapstick comedy to high drama, from wartime exploits to romantic liaisons, from light-hearted musicals to high-tech science fiction and just about everything in between. Films were awarded certificates by the British Board of Film Censors, according to age groups for which they thought the films suitable, or unsuitable. The U certificate meant a film could be watched by the whole family. The A certificate signified that children could watch the film but only in the company of an adult. Up until the start of the decade the H certificate was awarded to horror films, but in 1951, this was superseded by the X certificate, meaning no one under the age of 16 could be admitted.

Here are some of the different types of film that cinema audiences of the decade enjoyed.

War films: With the Second World War over by little more than four years at the start of the decade, it didn't take long for film-makers on both sides of the Atlantic to begin making films influenced by stories of the conflict. Some were based on true events, others with rather more romanticised versions of the facts. Offerings from British film-makers included *The Dam Busters (1955)*, *The Colditz Story* (1955), *Cockleshell Heroes* (1956) and *Reach For The Sky* (1956) to name but four. In all, more than 250 war films, produced principally by British and American studios, reached British cinema screens during the decade.

Biblical epics: If you want a good story, turn to the Bible. That seemed to be the message taken up by many film producers of the 1950s, mostly in America, but with films soon to be seen in Britain. The decade kicked off with *Samson and Delilah*, made in 1949, but seen on general release in Britain in 1950. It was followed by epic films that included *Quo Vadis* (1951), *The Robe* (1953), *The Ten Commandments* (1956) and *Ben-Hur* (1959).

Science fiction: Nearly 200 science fictions films found their way onto British cinema screens during the 1950s. It was a golden age for the genre at a time when special effects in films were beginning to achieve far more realism than in the past. Film-makers, therefore, had no problem taking audiences into space to visit alien planets, or to depict flying saucers landing in more familiar Earth locations. Films ranged from cringingly awful productions like *Plan 9 From Outer Space* (1957) to spectacular classics like *This Island Earth* (1955) and *Forbidden Planet* (1956), taking in along the way the rather more laughable *Invaders From Mars* (1953) and the eerie *Invasion of the Body Snatchers* (1956).

The poster for *The Ten Commandments*, heralded as 'the greatest event in motion picture history'.

Horror: There was a subtle crossover between science fiction and horror films of the 1950s. The difference was in the way science fiction depicted what might be possible with plots that were rarely meant to frighten audiences, while horror films were more likely to depict the impossible with stories expressly designed to scare. The Hammer studio dominated horror film production throughout the decade. Founded in 1934, Hammer made everything from comedy to intense dramas throughout the 1930s and 1940s. Then, in 1955, the studio made a film adaptation of the television classic *The Quatermass Experiment*, changing one word in the title from *Experiment* to *Xperiment* to play on the notoriety of the X certificate. It changed the course of history for Hammer, which went on to produce such classics as *The Curse of Frankenstein* (1957) with lavish sets and elaborate costumes filmed in blood-curdling colour, followed by further classics such as *The Abominable Snowman* (1957), *Horror of Dracula* (1958) and *The Mummy* (1959), all of which spawned equally over-the-top and ever-more frightening sequels.

Robby the Robot strides across an alien landscape in the poster for *Forbidden Planet*.

Musicals: In a climate of rationing and austerity, many cinema audiences of the 1950s craved something light-hearted and frothy. They got it with American musicals like *Hans Christian Anderson* (1952), *Seven Brides for Seven Brothers* (1954), *Oklahoma!* (1955), *Carousel* (1956) and *The King and I* (1956), the last three with music and lyrics by Richard Rodgers and Oscar Hammerstein who went on to score *The Sound of Music*, one of the most popular musicals ever, made as a film in 1965. The British film industry, so adept at producing other genres of film, failed to keep pace with the American output. With a few weak exceptions like *The Duke Wore Jeans* (1958) and *Idol on Parade* (1959), the British film industry, which had released a few notable musicals in the 1930s and 1940s, largely skipped the genre in the 1950s and didn't produce anything of note until the likes of *A Hard Day's Night*, *Oliver!* and *Oh! What a Lovey War* in the 1960s.

Comedy: The Ealing Studios were at the top of their game with 1950s film comedies, but they were not alone. The slapstick comedian Norman Wisdom, who worked initially with Two Cities Films and later with The Rank Organisation, was known for a series of budget black-and-white films that included *Trouble In Store* (1953), *The Square Peg* (1959), *Follow a Star* (1959), and many more which continued into the 1960s. The end of the 1950s also marked the start of one of the most popular ever British comedy film franchises. *Carry on Sergeant* (1959), made by Peter Rogers Productions, was a comedy about national service. It was never intended to be part of a series, but nevertheless turned out to be the first of a hugely successful succession of more than thirty comic films – mostly starring the same actors at the head of the cast – that kept *Carry On* in the title, all the way into the 1970s. One last resurrection of the franchise in 1992 saw *Carry on Columbus* made to celebrate the 500th anniversary of Christopher Columbus's discovery of the Americas.

Drama: Although British film-makers found themselves at home with comedy, early films of the decade struggled with serious drama. With a few exceptions such as *The Browning Version* (1951), not to mention a plethora of B-picture detective stories, most of the dramatic films that reached British cinemas at this time were made in America. Then, in 1958, British dramatic cinema took a new turn with the release of *Look Back in Anger*, made by

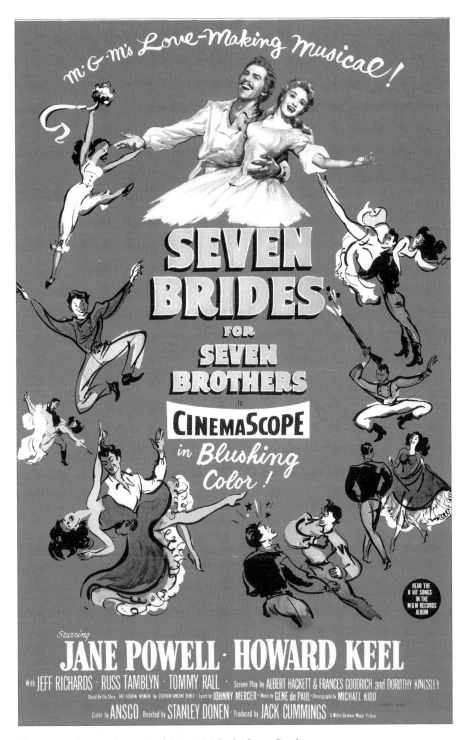

The poster for popular musical *Seven Brides for Seven Brothers*.

British Woodfall Film Productions. The plot concerned a love triangle between a dissatisfied working-class man, his snobbish middle-class wife and her best friend, whom the husband hates but with whom he eventually has an affair. Based on a play by John Osborne, it marked the start of what became known as the kitchen sink drama, a genre which, for the rest of the decade and into the 1960s, flourished in films, television plays and novels. The protagonists in all these stories were shown as young men disillusioned with the society in which they were forced to live, their type characterised by the new expression 'angry young men'. The film poster for *Look Back in Anger* quoted one critic of the film as saying, 'The audience was jolted as if they'd been sitting for two hours in an electric chair.'

Foreign films: Cinema audiences often attending for the sake of going to the pictures on a weekly basis, rather than waiting around to see a specific film, were often surprised to see the curtains go back on a main feature with actors speaking in a foreign language. Thus, foreign films like Jacques Tati's *Les Vacances de Monsieur Hulot* (1953) and *Mon Oncle* (1958), or Federico Fellini's *Las Strada* (1954) and *Le notti di Cabiria* (1957) found their way onto the weekly cinema circuit. Even Spanish films like *Los Olvidados* (1950) or Japanese productions such as *Rashomon* (1951) or *Seven Samurai* (1954) had their week of fame in British cinemas at a time when audiences were more prepared to read subtitles than might be the case with most cinema audiences today.

The making of an epic

It's impossible to pick out one film that epitomised the 1950s more than any other. But there is one which, although American in origin, stood head and shoulders above most others of the decade for British cinema audiences in terms of its sheer spectacle. With a running time of three hours forty-four minutes, forty minutes of which were taken up with a spectacular chariot race, and a budget of $15 million (the equivalent of about $140 million today), the film was *Ben-Hur*.

The film told the story of Judah Ben-Hur, a member of a Jewish noble family living in Rome who is betrayed and sent into slavery by a Roman friend, but who gains his freedom and returns for revenge, meeting Jesus Christ on the way.

Following in the footsteps of *The Ten Commandments* three years before, *Ben-Hur* took British cinemas by storm. Filmed in a special format known as *MGM Camera 65*, its pre-release ran at the Empire cinema in London's Leicester Square, where the film's extra-wide screen wowed audiences for months before it was given a general release to local cinemas all over the UK. Here are a dozen facts that those audiences might not have been aware of:

1. The film was actually a remake of a black-and-white silent film made in 1925.
2. Charlton Heston, so iconic in the leading role, was far from the first actor to be offered the part. Among those who turned it down were Burt Lancaster, Paul Newman, Marlon Brando, Rock Hudson and Kirk Douglas.
3. There were 365 speaking parts in the film.
4. Production required approximately 1 million props, 100,000 costumes, 1 million pounds of plaster and 40,000 cubic feet of wood.
5. Opera singer Claude Heater played the role of Jesus, but his face was never shown and he was not mentioned in the film's credits.
6. What was then the biggest film set ever built was constructed for the chariot race, the film's highlight sequence. It consisted of a stadium five storeys high around a race track that was 2,000 feet long and 65 feet wide.
7. For the race, seventy-eight horses were imported from Yugoslavia and Sicily. Contrary to stories of the time, none was injured.
8. Around 10,000 extras were employed throughout the film, 1,500 alone for the days when the chariot race was being filmed.
9. Urban myth claimed several stuntmen had been killed by trampling horses during the race; in fact, the only thing trampled by the horses were realistic dummies.
10. Music for the film, written by Miklós Rózsa, at 110 minutes, was the longest film music score ever composed.
11. The familiar roaring lion that marked the start of all MGM movies was silenced out of reverence for the nativity scene that began the film.
12. Later, in 1972, leftover footage from the film's sea battle was used in a film version of *Antony and Cleopatra*.

The poster that advertised *Ben-Hur* to British cinema audiences.

A popular joke of the 1950s went like this:

> 'I saw *Ben-Hur* last night.'
> 'Did you enjoy it?'
> 'Loved Ben, hated her.'

Wider and deeper

The 1950s saw a number of revolutions in the way films were made and shown. Three-dimensional technology, popularly known as 3D, made a brief impact with films that appeared to show everything with a new sense of depth and objects that appeared to fly off the screen straight at the audience. The technology that made this happen relied on a double image on the screen, one red and one green, and, in order to see everything in three dimensions, audience members were forced to wear what were known as anaglyph spectacles. These were actually little more than pieces of cardboard with two 'lenses' made from thin sheets of transparent plastic, one red and the other green. The technology was popular with science fiction makers in films like *Invaders From Mars* (1953), shot with deliberately distorted perspectives that emphasised the effect. Before the brief craze died out, at least one musical – *Kiss Me Kate* (1953) – was also shot in 3D.

Then came widescreen. It began with Cinerama, first seen in 1952, which was originally shot on three synchronised cameras side by side before being projected onto a curved screen by three interlocked projectors. The screen was so wide that it covered the viewer's peripheral vision to the extent that, when sitting looking directly at the centre of the screen, the viewer could see nothing else but the screen. An early film shot in Cinerama involved a rollercoaster ride, shot from the viewpoint of the first coach. It was not unheard of for audiences to scream while watching it and stories were told of people who actually vomited during the performance. Later, the Cinerama name was retained for a less ambitious system that used 65mm film in a single camera.

The problem with Cinerama was that it could not be projected by conventional projectors, and films shot in Cinerama failed to provide the same impact when they reached local cinemas. The arrival of Cinemascope was a lot more practical in terms of projection, requiring nothing more

Anaglyph red and green spectacles that cinema audiences needed to wear to see films in 3D.

than the addition of a simple accessory to the projector in the shape of an anamorphic lens, plus a new extra-wide screen. Audiences who had sat through the evening's second feature and newsreel viewed in a conventional screen format were astonished when the curtains across the screen went back after the interval, because they didn't stop where most expected them

From *This Is Cinerama*, the moving image was projected onto the screen by three synchronised projectors.

to stop, but just kept going to reveal a new super-wide screen. A Biblical epic *The Robe* was the first feature film made with the new technology and released in 1953. CinemaScope dominated film production for the rest of the decade and well into the next, but it had its rivals.

VistaVision in 1953 ran the film sideways through the camera to record a larger and wider size image on film for projection in specially designed projectors, or printed onto a normal width 35mm frame for projection in conventional equipment. Todd-AO in 1954 used special cameras that took 75mm wide film in place of 35mm.

Not that the theory behind any of this new technology had any serious impact on audiences. They didn't really want to know how the films were brought to the screen. They were just happy to know that some films, particularly early in the decade, were in black and white; later films were more likely to be in colour; some were in a conventional format; others were super-wide; and occasionally they were in three dimensions. It was all part of the weekly experience of simply going to the pictures in the 1950s.

Chapter 11

Road, Rail and Air Travel

The British motor industry – trams – motor buses – trolleybuses
– the demise of steam railways – the golden age of air travel

FACT BOX

- In 1950, about 3 million people owned cars in Britain.
- Car ownership was made more feasible for many by Ford.
- Advertisements of the time were often condescending towards women drivers.
- Trams ran on metal rails embedded into the streets.
- It was considered normal to get on and off buses at traffic lights.
- Women bus conductors were known as clippies.
- Trolleybuses picked up an electric current to run their engines from overhead wires.
- Until 1956, railway carriages were designated only as First Class and Third Class, with no Second Class.
- The British-made Comet was the world's first jet airliner.

In the 1950s, travelling around was a lot more complicated than simply walking out of your front door, jumping into your car and going where you needed to be. Private car ownership in Britain in 1950 was about 3 million, a figure that would only just about double by the end of the decade. In 1959, the price of an Austin A35, which was a small family car, was £538. A Hillman Minx, which was a little larger and more luxurious, cost £750. Rolls-Royce cars started at £5,387.

Side streets in those days were devoid of parked cars and vehicles moving along them were few. So much so that, in most towns, children could play safely in the side streets, rolling marbles along gutters, carefully avoiding the drains, of course, and frequently setting up cricket pitches down the

Although the year is 1956, the Wolseley 9 car dates from 1935 and the 1950s road is empty and clear enough for father and son to work on repairs.

centre of the road, moving respectfully aside on the rare occasions that a vehicle needed to pass.

For much of the 1950s, short journeys undertaken for most involved walking to the nearest main road and taking a bus, or walking much further to the nearest station and catching a train. In the early years at least, hardly anyone knew anyone else who had ever been on an aeroplane.

It was by no means unusual for drivers in the mid-1950s to be driving cars built before the Second World War.

The British motor industry

Although there were plenty of new cars manufactured even in the early 1950s, those who were lucky enough to own a car were likely to be driving one that had been bought second-hand and which dated back to before the Second World War. Cars made in the 1930s were popular among drivers of the 1950s, which meant they were inevitably unreliable, reluctant to start and prone to breaking down. It was why most car owners were also amateur motor mechanics.

A 1937 open-top Austin 10 Greyhound in London's Piccadilly Circus in 1951. The driver and his wife had driven this car all the way from North Wales for the Festival of Britain celebrations.

Ford

The company that more than any other made car ownership viable was Ford. It was an American company whose first production car was the Model A in 1903, going on to win much acclaim for the production of the

15 miles from South Bank Exhibition

ONCE it was a lonely riverside marsh with tall reeds shifted by the winds. Today —a mighty factory stands there, employing 16,000 people. There, the Ford cars you know so well are built . . . there, the big tough Thames Trucks—the sturdy Thames Vans and the famous Fordson Major Tractors are turned out minute by minute. To the far corners of the world these Ford products go. They stand the rigours of every climate, they give a fine performance—always reliable— always economical. And they are, every one, backed by the incomparable Ford Dealer Service which spans the globe.

BY APPOINTMENT TO
H M KING GEORGE VI
MOTOR VEHICLE
MANUFACTURERS

FORD MOTOR COMPANY LIMITED · DAGENHAM

The Ford factory at Dagenham, as shown in a 1951 advertisement for the company.

Model T in 1908. At the start, Ford made cars one at a time, but it was the development of mass production that saw them reap the most benefits from the growing motor car ownership market. In 1929, construction began on Britain's and Europe's largest car plant. The site chosen for the enormous British factory was Dagenham, then a town in Essex and now a London borough. The factory opened in 1931 with a great many of its workers moving into the nearby Becontree Estate, once described as the largest housing estate in the world.

As with so many other manufacturers, the Second World War saw Ford turn its resources to the war effort. But with the end of the war, commercial car production began in earnest and by the 1950s, as car ownership grew, newly affluent drivers began buying Ford cars like the Anglia, whose original model was made from 1940 until 1953. This was a small, box-shaped car with two doors, but seats for a family of four, two of whom would have entered the back by tipping the front seats forward. For the person who could afford something more lavish, there was the Ford V8 Pilot that had been around since 1947. The Ford Zephyr Six,

The early style of the Ford Anglia.

For the 1950s, a very modern-looking Ford Zephyr.

made from 1950 until 1954, was particularly attractive with a smaller British style that echoed much larger American cars of the day. The smooth body design did away with the running boards that had been a design mainstay of most cars until then.

The similarly designed Ford Consul followed in 1951 and was made until 1962. In 1953, the Anglia was remodelled. Moving away from the

The newly styled Ford Anglia with its unusual sloping rear window.

boxy design with little boot space, it now became a smaller version of the style already popularised by the Zephyr and Consul with a compartment for four people, a long flat bonnet in front and a larger-than-usual boot at the rear. In 1959, the Anglia was redesigned yet again as the Model 105E to make one of Ford's most iconic small cars with its sloping front end and unusual backward-slanted rear window devised to keep it clear in rain. Other Ford cars produced during the 1950s included the Popular, similar in style to the early Anglias; the Prefect, a slightly more upmarket version of the Anglia and Popular; and the Zodiac, a luxury variant of the Zephyr.

British Motor Corporation

Ford's biggest rival at this time was the British Motor Corporation (BMC). The company grew out of the amalgamation of prestigious names that included Morris, Wolseley, Riley and MG. Riley was a company whose origins dated back to 1899, but by 1938 was getting into financial difficulties. In that year, Riley was taken over by motor engineer and philanthropist Lord Nuffield and amalgamated with the company whose name stemmed from his own – William Richard Morris. Morris Motors had been around since 1919, but the company soon became known as the Nuffield Organisation, then almost immediately turned production over to supporting the war effort during the Second World War. When the war ended in 1945, car production began again but in 1952 a merger was agreed with the Austin company to form BMC, which served the popular car industry during the rest of the decade for those drivers who considered Ford's cars perhaps a little too mass produced for their tastes. BMC cars bought during the 1950s included the Morris Six, Morris Oxford, Morris Minor, MG 1¼ litre saloon, MG TD, Wolseley 6/90, Wolseley 4/50, Riley RMA, RMB and RME.

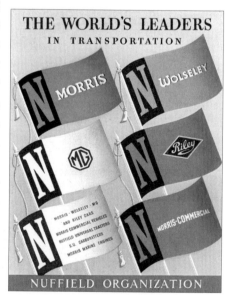

A Nuffield advertisement from 1961.

Three classics of the 1950s. Top to bottom: 1953 MG TD, 1954 Riley RME and 1957 Morris Minor.

One of BMC's most iconic successes came right at the end of the decade. In 1959, the company introduced the Mini, originally marketed in two versions: the Morris Mini-Minor (a reference to the larger Morris Minor) and the Austin 7 (a throwback to the name of one of the Austin company's cars from the 1920s and 1930s). The styles of the two Minis were near enough identical, apart from their name badges and front grills. Designed by BMC's top engineer Alec Issigonis, the Mini stemmed from Britain's need at that time for a more fuel-efficient car. Its design began with an 848cc engine and gearbox that were positioned sideways across the car, allowing for front-wheel drive and an engine weight over the front wheels that increased stability. The car measured only a little more than 10ft long, 4ft 7in wide and 4ft 5in high, with a ground clearance of just 6 inches. Sliding windows were used in place of the usual roll-down types. With its four wheels positioned at the extreme edges of the body, the engine space kept to a minimum and only a small boot, the inside dimensions were surprisingly roomy for four adults. Following its initial launch as a two-door saloon, a three-door estate was produced in 1960, followed by vans, pick-ups, convertibles and the sporty Mini Cooper, which arrived in 1961. The marque still survives today. Although the cars still carry the Mini name, they are no longer mini in size.

Born in the 1950s and destined to become an icon of the 1960s: the Morris Mini Minor.

Other prestigious makes

Meanwhile, at the other end of the market, luxury cars were being built, even if they were only bought by the few. Jaguar, Daimler and even Rolls-Royce were regularly advertised in magazines aimed at people on average incomes. But so too were marques that are now largely forgotten. There was Humber, for example, which by the end of the 1950s was producing 200,000 cars a year. The range included large luxury vehicles like the Hawk and Super Snipe. But when the company was faced with building a small family car called the Hillman Imp in the 1960s as a rival to the Mini, it was found wanting and was eventually absorbed by the Chrysler Corporation in 1967. Then there was Frazer Nash, making sports cars like the Mille Miglia, Targa Florio, Le Mans Coupé and the Sebring before ceasing manufacture in 1957. And there was Rover, whose cars were made at Solihull in Warwickshire, with a luxury range that included the popular Rover 90, made between 1954 and 1969. Rover continued to make its executive-styled cars until the company was sold to British Leyland in 1967. Jowett Cars began manufacture at Bradford in Yorkshire in 1906. Between 1947 and 1953, the company produced an executive car called the Javelin, rakishly designed with a sloping back that made it stand out against other cars of the day. 'Take a good look when it passes you,' said the advertising, which briefly summed up its specification like this: 'Top speed, electrically timed, 78mph. Acceleration 0-60mph in 22.2 seconds. Horizontally opposed flat-four 50 BHP engine.'

Armstrong Siddeley was another now largely forgotten name, this time with a background in the aircraft industry, which led to aircraft-like names for some of its cars, such as the Hurricane and Lancaster before ceasing manufacture in 1960. Advertisements for Lancaster illustrate how times have changed in the political correctness of advertising. Showing a man and a woman seemingly in deep discussion, the advert consisted of dialogue that went something like this ...

'Of course women are difficult to please.'

'Starting an argument, Jim?'

'No, stating facts. Take cars. A woman's not satisfied with fine engineering. Tell her about automatic chassis lubrication or why a down draft carburettor saves fuel – ten to one she'll not be listening.'

'Quite a speech, Jim. Yet you're quite wrong about feminine taste. Now what I call a perfect car ...'

giving away some litres

You're a very moderate driver — so you always say. There's no hurry, 40 gets you there as quickly as 60.

But then, as that bigger-engined car bundles past, something in you puts more pressure on the throttle. The Javelin responds instantly. You re-pass.

But you've taken on a powerful opponent. You sit a little straighter in your seat — glance in the driving mirror. Yes, he's there.

You're cruising fast now, snicking into top after maximum in third. And you love the way she behaves. Gripping the corners as if on rails.

Nearly flat-out and perfectly in control — wheel rock-steady; brakes seeming just to suck you back and the torsion bar suspension cushioning the road.

You keep it up for quite a time. But on the straight he passes you finally. You knew he would, but you're happy — with a 1½ litre family saloon you held all his litres. And that little bit of fun didn't run away with your petrol — the Javelin's an economical car even at speed.

This car is a waste of money if you don't care what a car does. There's such a lot built into it that doesn't really show until you have it in your hands — performance, comfort and 30 m.p.g.

Top speed, electrically timed, 78 m.p.h. Acceleration 0-60 m.p.h. in 22.2 secs. ("The Motor" Road Test.) Horizontally opposed flat-four 50 B.H.P. Engine. Javelin saloon £635 plus purchase tax Javelin saloon de luxe £735 plus purchase tax.

A 1951 advertisement for the Jowett Javelin.

Luxury driving, 1950s-style, from Jaguar and Daimler.

'Here it comes.'

'... a perfect car is one that's simple to drive, comfy, roomy, warm but not drafty and ...'

'Hey stop! Are you talking about the new Lancaster Fourteen?'

'Of course, dear. Everyone is.'

'Now that's wonderful. It has so many new features.'

Trams, trolleys and buses

Trams

A London Transport tram in Tooley Street.

Although there are towns and cities in Britain that still successfully run modern tram services, the type of vehicle that epitomised a tram of the early twentieth century was on its way out by the start of the 1950s. There were different styles, but most followed a similar layout: a two-deck vehicle with seats for passengers on the lower deck and on an upstairs deck accessed by stairways at each end of the vehicle. The seats were usually made of wood, known for being hard and uncomfortable.

Trams had flanged wheels like railway engines and their carriages, and they ran on rails like railway lines, the difference being that these rails were embedded in everyday streets. Although, in the past, trams had been horse-drawn, driven by steam and even gas, those that still survived into the 1950s were powered by about 600 volts of electricity delivered from an overhead wire, via a single pole on the roof of the tram, with the current being harmlessly returned to earth through the rails.

Trams were difficult to turn around, other than by use of a turntable in the ground at the depot, so many used a system of two driving cabs, one

Tramlines were embedded into the street.

Hanwell to Brentford tram in London's Boston Road.

at each end of the vehicle. When the tram reached the end of the line, the pole that picked up the overhead power was rotated through 180 degrees, then the driver simply walked from one end of the tram to the other, took his seat in the second cab and drove it back in the opposite direction. For a similar reason, the seats often had backs that swivelled so they could be adjusted for passengers to face forwards or backwards.

Because the rails only completed the electrical circuit, there was no danger to people in the street stepping on them. However, if a tram happened to come off the rails, or was stalled because of some substance covering the rails and therefore preventing completion of the electrical circuit, then there was serious danger to passengers and nearby pedestrians. If the pole was still in contact with the overheard live wire, the current was still live in parts of the tram's metal body. If someone stepped off the tram, while still holding on to some part of it, or if someone in the road touched the tram, their body completed the electrical circuit, especially if the road was wet, and the person could then receive a severe electric shock. If a tram became stalled in this way, the driver was required to jump off immediately, while avoiding contact with the tram's metal bodywork,

A tram crash which has led to a build-up of other trams behind that have no way of passing.

and to pull down the overhead pole from the wire above, cutting off the electricity to the body of the tram.

Another problem was that since every tram's precise route was restricted to the rails, it was unable to steer around any obstacles in its path. As more manoeuvrable cars began to appear on the roads, the inflexibility of the way trams travelled began to make them a liability. Worse still, if a tram broke down, there was no way for those following to steer around it, causing a tailback of stationary trams along the rails and inevitably leading to even more congestion. The last London tram ran in 1952 and others were phased out around the country during the 1950s. They were replaced by motor buses and, very often, trolleybuses.

Motor buses

Boarding, travelling on and getting off buses in the 1950s was something of an art, now long forgotten. First consider the design of the average bus. Although there were single-decker buses travelling on many of the country's routes, the design that summed up the word 'bus' for most was that of the double-decker. And the bus that typified the double-decker in the 1950s was the RT. Manufactured from 1939 until the mid-1950s, the RT, whose initials actually stood for 'Regent Three', was built by the Associated Equipment Company (AEC). The bus is chiefly remembered in its red livery for London Transport. But between 1946 and 1951, AEC sold RT chassis, onto which different bus companies built their own bodies in their own liveries, to operators in places that included Aberdeen, Birmingham, Coventry, Devon, Glasgow, Grimsby, Halifax, Rhondda, St Helens and West Riding. If you boarded a bus almost anywhere in the country during the 1950s, it's likely that somewhere in its heavy metal body beat the heart of an RT.

The bus was 26ft long, 7ft 6in wide and 14ft 5in high. The driver sat in a cab at the front, accessed by his own door and completely separated from the passengers. Every bus also had a conductor. The bus held fifty-six passengers distributed over the two decks. Entrance was from the rear. There were no doors, just sturdy handles on each side of a boarding platform and a pole in its centre. The stairs were on the right of the platform and curved round as they climbed to the top deck. There was a place under the stairs where passengers could stow items like parcels and small prams. Smoking was allowed on the top deck, and so too were dogs, though getting big dogs up and down the narrow stairs was not easy. Neither smoking nor dogs were allowed on the lower deck, though it was permissible for five people to stand in the lower deck aisle between the double seats when the bus was full. Standing was not allowed on the top deck.

Passengers boarded buses at bus stops, and there were two types. At compulsory stops the driver was obliged to stop every time, irrespective of if there were new passengers to get on or existing ones to get off. At request stops, the driver did not have to stop unless a waiting passenger leaned out into the road and stuck out his or her hand. Those inside the bus wanting to get off were required to ring a bell in the driver's compartment. This was carried out by tugging on a cord that ran the length of the ceiling of the lower deck, or by pushing a button high up on the platform. Passengers were only allowed to push the button or pull the cord once for a single 'ding', which meant stop. Two 'dings' meant go, but woe betide any passenger who tried this. Only the conductor was allowed to give the bell two 'dings'. With a conductor in charge of everything but the actual driving, and with drivers therefore freed up from having to take fares, boarding a bus was speeded up, especially important when so many bus stops had long queues of people waiting for the arrival of the next bus.

The RT as a London Transport bus.

The rear platform where passengers boarded and left most double-decker buses of the 1950s.

After the driver, the conductor was the most important person on the bus. During the Second World War, when men were away fighting, women took over conductor duties. After the war, in the early 1950s, some women were still employed by bus companies, but by and large, conductors were men. All conductors had uniforms, usually dark navy blue or sometimes dark green, with peaked caps, and they wore badges on lapels and caps indicating individual bus companies. The conductors travelled on the platform beside the stairs, controlling how passengers got on and off the bus and preventing further people from boarding when the bus was full, before giving the bell its two 'dings' to indicate to the driver that he could safely move away.

Once the bus was in motion, the conductor made his way along the aisle taking fares. The fare varied according to where a passenger got on and where he or she intended to get off. Passengers held out their money and told the conductor their destinations. The strange thing was that even if the conductor didn't get round to taking a fare from someone until they were a good way past the stop where they had boarded, he always seemed to remember where each individual passenger had got onto the bus and so knew how much to charge.

In the early years, tickets of various denominations were held in a wooden rack behind a wire clip. The conductor would remove the appropriate one and put it in the ticket clipping machine hanging around his neck. As he pressed a lever to punch a hole in an appropriate place to indicate the journey's destination, the machine rang a soft bell. Money was dropped into a leather satchel also worn around the conductor's neck and over a shoulder. Because of the ticket clipping action, women conductors were affectionately known as clippies; men were never referred to in this way. Later, the individual tickets in a rack were replaced by another machine that the conductor wore around his neck. With the money taken, he dialled in a price on a wheel on the top of the machine, or a knob on the side, and turned a handle, whereupon the ticket, in the form of a printed strip of paper, would emerge from a slot to be torn off and handed to the passenger. The conductor's other task was to change the destination boards at the front and back of the bus when it arrived at the depot, before it moved off for a return journey. The details were in the form of white lettering on tough black cloth unrolled from one roller and wound on to another.

A bus conductor's ticket machine.

Although bus stops were the places where people were officially supposed to board or alight from a bus, it was by no means unusual for people to hop on or off at traffic lights or while the bus was moving, preferably when it slowed down for some reason such as taking a corner. Although this was officially illegal, it was perfectly acceptable and rare for a conductor to stop it happening. Boarding a bus while it was moving involved running hard to match its speed, then grabbling the handle at the back of the platform and jumping on. Getting off a moving bus needed a little more skill. The knack was to first wait until the bus was moving as slowly as possible, then while holding the handle at the back of the platform to let go and step off backwards, hitting the ground running or at least at a fast walking pace. Stepping forward off the back of a moving bus could be disastrous.

The RT and its variations of model epitomised bus travel throughout the 1950s, but there was another bus that was specially designed and built during the decade that many a passenger will claim to have been the best bus ever. It was called the Routemaster. Designed by and for London Transport, the company that ran buses in and around London at the time, the Routemaster was built by AEC. The first prototype was seen in 1954, but the bus, in the iconic shape that it thereafter became, didn't enter service until 1956. Its innovative design used lightweight aluminium and

Routemaster buses that began in the 1950s and continued though five decades.

building techniques learnt from aircraft production during the Second World War. For the first time, the driver and passengers had the benefit of a smoother ride that came with independent front suspension, power steering, an automatic gearbox and power hydraulic brakes. Like the RT before it, the driver's cab was at the front, cut off from passengers, while a platform at the back allowed fast boarding and leaving, as well as the opportunity to hop on or off at places other than official bus stops. The Routemaster was larger than its predecessor, at 27ft 6in long, 8ft wide and 14ft 5in high. Once again, the driver was teamed with a conductor, minimising boarding time, taking fares and keeping order among passengers that numbered sixty-four – twenty-eight downstairs and thirty-six upstairs – when the bus was full.

Although Routemasters were built for London Transport, a small number were also built for British European Airways and the Northern General Transport Company. The bus survived the privatisation of London Transport in the mid-1990s and the last Routemaster, in its well-known and well-loved 1950s design, ran until December 2005.

Trolleybuses

Double-decker trolleybuses in Maidstone (top) and Glasgow.

Trolleybuses were similar in size and shape to motor buses, sometimes single-deckers, but more often double-deckers, some styles having a total of six wheels, two at the front and four at the back. Having normal rubber tyres rather than metal wheels on rails like trams, trolleybuses could steer around obstacles. Unlike normal motor buses, however, they were electrically driven. Their power was picked up from a network of overhead cables, but they needed two wires, because they didn't have metal rails to complete the electric circuit as was the case with trams. Like motor buses, the driver's compartment was cut off from the passengers, and a conductor was on board to keep order and take fares.

Trolleybuses, already popular in mainland Europe, arrived in the UK in 1911 with Leeds and Bradford the first to operate fleets. By the 1950s there were around fifty fleets of trolleybuses running around the country, with London's red Central Area buses being the largest. Compared to

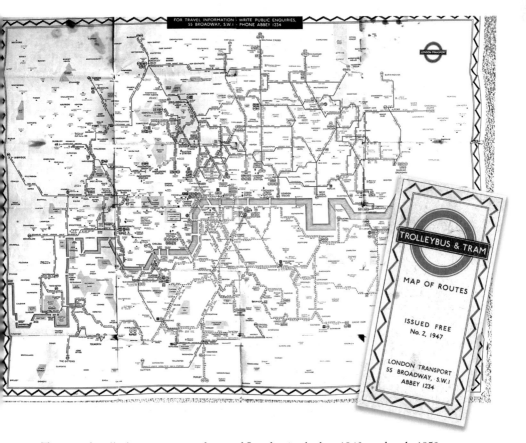

Trams and trolleybus routes in and around London in the late 1940s and early 1950s.

a motor bus, they had a flat front with no sign of a bonnet to house the engine. They ran smoothly and – thanks to the electric, rather than petrol or diesel engine – almost silently.

Some of the trolleybuses on London Transport's Central Area routes had tinted windows. This was because those vehicles had originally been built for use in South Africa. The Leyland company built twenty-five for Durban, while AEC had made eighteen for use in Johannesburg. But the Second World War had intervened and the buses ended up in 1950s London, where the tinted windows, made to reduce the glare of the South African sun, were less appropriate. These trolleybuses were built with front exits for use in South Africa, although those exits had been sealed up and replaced by a sideways seat by the time they started working on the London Transport routes. Entry and exit was by the usual red London bus means of a rear platform with a pole in the middle to hang on to.

Towns and cities that ran trolleybus routes erected complicated networks of overhead wires from which the vehicles picked up their electric current via the twin poles extending from the roof. Junctions where different bus numbers took different routes necessitated a set of points for the overhead

A single-deck trolleybus operating in Glasgow.

wires that worked much like those on a railway track, usually operated by pulling a large brass knob that protruded from a box on one of the wire-supporting poles. To ensure every bus went in the right direction they were often run in a strict rotation with a specific bus number always following another. In this way, the conductor of each bus could reach out from his place on the rear platform and change the points ready for the next bus.

A driver and conductor reattach the poles of a London trolleybus to the overhead wires.

Failure to operate the points in time for the following bus, or at other times when a driver took a bend too sharply, resulted in the poles coming adrift from the wires, leaving them flailing about in the air. That was when the driver and conductor took on extra duties as pole catchers. Together they removed a long pole from under the bus and, wrestling it in into an upright position, they hooked the poles and reattached them to the overhead wires before continuing their journey.

The reign of the trolleybus was relatively short-lived, with most being withdrawn, in London at least, by the end of the 1950s and the start of the 1960s. That left more than twenty other locations that ran services around Britain until the early 1970s. They were replaced by diesel motor buses, often Routemasters.

Railways

Steam railways began in the Britain during the Victorian age (1837–1901) and, by the 1950s, as far as technology was concerned, they had not really progressed very much from then. Many a young boy grew up with the ambition to be a train driver, failing to understand the difference between what was often referred to as the romance of steam and the tough reality of putting it to work. Being a train driver was difficult, cold and filthy work. It required a knowledge of how – in simplistic terms – heated water produced steam and how that steam put pressure on pistons that turned wheels. The number of controls needed to keep that pressure going, without allowing it to overlap into the danger zone, was far more skilful than passengers realised. And all the while the driver was watching and adjusting the controls that made this happen, his fireman, in the cab beside him, was shovelling coal into the furnace that heated the water and produced the steam. His was another back-breaking job.

To board a train passengers had to first buy a ticket at the ticket booth and then, before being allowed onto the station platform, to present the ticket to the ticket collector at a barrier who would not allow anyone any further without the appropriate ticket. At the other end of the journey, the same ticket had to be presented to another ticket collector before passengers were allowed off the platform and into the station's main concourse. Train spotters, or anyone who wanted to meet or say goodbye

Birmingham Snow Hill Station in the late 1950s.

to a passenger, could purchase, for the price of one penny, a platform ticket that entitled them to go onto the platform, but not to board a train.

When it came to boarding the train, there were two types of carriage. The most common type, which would often be found on local short-haul runs, consisted of compartments situated across the width of the carriage with a door at each end, corresponding to the two sides of the carriage. This meant that each compartment in a carriage could be entered from one side or the other, depending on how the train entered the station and therefore which side faced the platform. The doors were known as slam doors, and they were opened and closed manually by an outside handle. Each of the compartments had a bench seat that ran along both sides

Acocks Green and South Yardley station in May 1957.

of its width. Above the seats, webbing on metal struts constituted the luggage rack. Once passengers were inside one of these compartments and the train had begun to move, they were there for the duration of the journey. There was nowhere else to go. The windows were strange affairs. They travelled up and down, and there were leather belts strung beneath them with notches to slip over studs beneath the window frames. Pulling hard on one of these belts caused the window to go up and the degree of opening was controlled by which notch was used to fasten the belt in place. Loosening the belt caused the window to drop back down. When passengers arrived at their destinations, it wasn't uncommon to discover a lack of opening handle on the inside of the door,

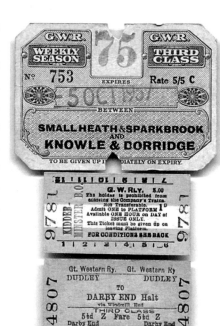

Top to bottom: a season ticket, a platform ticket and a Third Class travel ticket.

or a sliding mechanism that was so stiff it was impossible to operate it. In that case the window was lowered, a passenger leaned out of the window and unlatched the door using the outside handle.

Carriages used on longer journeys also placed compartments across the width of the carriage, but one end of the compartment, rather than leading to the outside, led to a corridor that ran the length of the train. Passengers, then, were free to wander up and down the corridor, to visit other compartments, to use the toilet which was situated at the end of most corridor carriages, to buy a drink, sandwich or cake at a snack bar, or to even partake of a full three-course meal served in the restaurant car.

The last carriage was likely to be the guard's van. Here, large parcels or items like bikes could be left for the duration of a journey. It was also the place where the guard travelled. His job was to get off the train at each stop, to watch as passengers alighted and boarded and, when everyone was on board and all the carriage doors were shut, to wave a flag to indicate to the driver that it was safe to move off.

Most trains had two classes of carriage which passengers were allowed to use depending on which ticket had been bought, one class being a little more luxurious, and with a higher ticket price, than the other. Incongruously they were identified as First Class and Third Class. This was because in the early days of rail travel there had been three classes, logically called First, Second and Third. But in the nineteenth century, most railways abandoned Second Class, so that by the first half of the 1950s, there was only First and Third, with nothing in between. In 1956, Third Class was renamed Second Class, an identity it retained until the 1980s, when it was renamed again as Standard Class.

Although they might not have been aware of it, passengers of the 1950s were travelling on railways that were somewhat inferior to those found in other parts of the world. While others were experimenting with diesel and electric technologies, Britain was stuck in the steam age.

In 1947, the railways in Britain had been nationalised under the British Transport Commission, which soon found that they were the proud owners of a system that had been severely damaged during the Second World War, and which was now dilapidated and in a dire financial state. As the 1950s began and progressed, discussions on modernisation took place and in 1955, a £1.2 billion plan was announced. It soon became clear, however, that a good half of what was a huge sum of money for

A diesel train in 1958, of the type that gradually began to replace steam.

those times would need to be spent merely on bringing the railways back to the way they had been in the past, and the other half put towards electrification in place of steam. Bearing in mind what was happening to railways in America and Europe, that seemed to be the way forward, but the scheme had its detractors. One economics advisor suggested to the Government that modernising the railways was a waste of money since people would rely on other means of transport, including their own personal helicopters, within thirty years. Others thought the cash would be better spent on the roads, where mass motoring was on the way.

In the end, the electrification plans were shelved and by the end of the 1950s, the only train types that replaced steam were cheaper, though largely untested, diesel engines. Some of these comprised little more than a locomotive chassis with a speed boat engine attached. It would be some years more before Britain's railways were electrified. There had been a time when steam represented a golden age. But even by the 1950s, it had become an age that had gone on just a little too long.

Air travel

The start of the 1950s marked the beginning of what is often described as the golden age of air travel, chiefly because, although few could afford to fly, those that could, did it in luxury. There was only one class, and that was First Class with as many extras as possible thrown in: free meals and drinks, and no objection to people who wished to smoke. For this, travellers paid in the region of £254 for a return to ticket to America. Airlines were conscious of the fact that if they wanted to attract more passengers, it would mean reducing fares, but the problem was that all fares were set at a fixed price for each type of journey by the International Air Traffic Association (IATA). It was only when Pan Am in America threatened to leave the IATA that things began to change. In Britain, airlines and the Government, attracted to the idea of bringing American

Travelling by air in the 1950s got off to a flying start in the first year of the decade, as the British-made Comet aeroplane emerged as the world's first commercial jet airliner. Built by the de Havilland company in Hertfordshire, its initial flight from London to Johannesburg set amazing new standards with speeds of up to 500 miles per hour and it was hailed as the start of a revolution in passenger air travel. The Comet was designed to fly higher than ever before, at speeds faster than ever before and, even though there were provisions on board for no more than thirty-six passengers, they would be guaranteed to travel in never before known luxury.

Comet prototype at de Havilland in Hertfordshire, where it was built.

Unfortunately, the Comet's success was short-lived. Over the next few years, a series of unexplained crashes revealed that the aircraft's shell was not strong enough to withstand the inevitable changes in air pressure. The Comet was grounded in 1954 and its place in history almost immediately taken over by the American airline Boeing with its 707 aircraft, developed from a Second World War B-52 bomber.

tourists and their dollars to Britain, also rebelled and, in 1952, Tourist Class was introduced for passengers who were happy to put up with a little less luxury. The fair for a return trip to America, for those travelling in Tourist Class, dropped to £173 13s, even then the kind of money that could buy a new car. Tourist Class was less comfortable than First Class, which still prevailed in another part of the plane, with 50 per cent more seats, leading to more cramped conditions. Passengers were also expected to pay for meals and no alcoholic drinks were served.

Despite these conditions, and the still high price of a seat, air travel gradually began to gain in popularity and, by 1957, Tourist Class made up 70 per cent of the fares charged. That same year, a third class was introduced. This one was called Economy Class, with prices 20 per cent cheaper than Tourist Class. This time, seats were placed closer together and meals were restricted to sandwiches with tea, coffee or mineral water. The only giveaways were boiled sweets for sucking during take-off and

Personal service to passengers when flying in the 1950s.

landing because it was believed that sucking a boiled sweet – in particular barley sugar – helped to prevent ears from 'popping' due to changes in air pressure. After that, a Deluxe service was offered that was even better than First Class, with passengers enjoying wide, reclining seats and gourmet food.

So, from a one-class only service at the start of the decade, in only a few years, airlines could offer four classes of service: Deluxe, First Class, Tourist and Economy, though it was rare for all four to be offered on the same plane. The four-class system didn't last long. By the end of the 1950s, it was far more common for an airline to offer only three classes. Such a three-class service, operated by the British Overseas Airways Corporation (BOAC) between London and New York on a DC-7 airliner, allowed for sixteen First Class seats, seventeen in Tourist and thirty-seven in Economy. Unlike today, the First Class seats were at the back of the plane, because that's where the doors were, allowing First Class passengers to disembark first.

The 1950s certainly saw air travel become more accessible, but it wasn't until the end of the decade that the average family could afford it, and even then, readily affordable seats were not among the most comfortable.

Chapter 12

Into a New Decade

How the 1950s evolved into the 1960s

Britain's transition from the 1950s into the 1960s was very different to the way the 1940s had led into the 1950s. The then current Prime Minister Harold Macmillan's assertion in 1957 that 'most of our people have never had it so good' was perhaps not entirely true. But the fact was that things were a lot better than ten years previously. The austerity endured through much of the 1950s was gone and, while few people would have called themselves rich, many were happy to lead comfortable lives that would have seemed positively luxurious compared to ten years before.

The National Health Service, which had been launched in 1948, had grown in stature throughout the 1950s and was, by 1960, firmly established and advancing, with lessons learnt from its inaugural years that would lead to an even better healthcare service in the years ahead. The previous decade had also seen a radical reduction in deaths from tuberculosis and polio.

Boys leaving school no longer faced the barrier of National Service taking a year and half out of their lives. A minority went to university, while the majority went straight into work, and the country pretty much enjoyed the benefit of full employment. The union movement that had grown in the 1950s had fought for decent wages and, for the first time, many people had a disposable income. As a result, foreign travel and holidays abroad became much more the norm.

By the end of the 1950s and into the first years of the 1960s, young people began to develop their own voices. They no longer took the lead from their parents when it came to fashion, music and general way of life. What became known as the Swinging Sixties was a time when so many threw off the shackles of conventions that they had unwittingly worn during the previous decade.

Change happened in the 1960s much faster than in the 1950s. But that isn't to say that the 1950s did not witness big changes in lifestyle, science, culture and more. Things just moved at a slower pace. It was a pace that many of those who grew up in the 1960s, but still with a foothold in and nostalgic memories of the 1950s, often found preferable and, in its own way and context, just a little bit more exciting.

Picture Credits

p. 2 NSSDC, NASA[1], Public domain, via Wikimedia Commons.

p. 4 British Government, Public domain, via Wikimedia Commons.

p. 6 From the collections of The National Archives via Wikimedia Commons.

pp. 9–10 Courtesy of Peter Hampson.

p. 11 Ministry of Information Photo Division Photographer, Public domain, via Wikimedia Commons.

pp. 12, 13 (top) Courtesy of the Butlin's Heritage Collection at the History of Advertising Trust (HAT) by kind permission of Bourne Leisure.

p. 13 (lower) From a contemporary postcard published by Valentine's.

p. 14 Public domain, via Wikimedia Commons.

p. 16 Courtesy of the Memorabilia Pack Company.

p. 17 Retrogasm, Public domain, via Wikimedia Commons.

p. 19 Courtesy of the Memorabilia Pack Company.

p. 20 Courtesy of Doghouse Vintage's Jack the Lad range.

p. 21 Courtesy of the Memorabilia Pack Company.

p. 22 (lower) Courtesy of Pat Rowley.

pp. 23–4 Courtesy of the Memorabilia Pack Company.

p. 27 Unknown author, Copyrighted free use, via Wikimedia Commons.

p. 28 Dave Snowden, CC BY-SA 2.0, via Wikimedia Commons.

p. 32 Sebastian F., CC BY-SA 3.0, via Wikimedia Commons.

p. 38 Courtesy of the Woolworths Museum (www.woolworthsmuseum.co.uk) © 3D and 6D pictures Ltd.

p. 43 Milestone Society, CC BY-SA 2.0 via Wikimedia Commons.

p. 52 Courtesy of Ron Holloway.

p. 55 Ministry of Information Photo Division Photographer, Public domain, via Wikimedia Commons.

p. 58 (top) Spaarnestad Photo, via Nationaal Archief, via Wikimedia Commons.

p. 58 (lower) Agriculture and Stock Department, Publicity Branch, via Wikimedia Commons.

p. 59 (top) Courtesy of John Rushton.

p. 62 Llyfrgell Genedlaethol Cymru, The National Library of Wales from Wales Cymru, via Wikimedia Commons.

p. 63 LlGC – NLW, via Wikimedia Commons.

pp. 70 (lower)–72 (top), 75–7, 79, 82, 84 Courtesy of Excalibur Auctions.

p. 85 Alfie-C, CC BY-SA 4.0, via Wikimedia Commons.

p. 93 (top) © Case Antiques Inc.

p. 96 From *The Illustrated London News*, 1851.

p. 97 Courtesy of James Styles.

pp. 101, 103–104, 105 From contemporary postcards, publishers unknown, courtesy of Keith Towel.

p. 107 From a 1951 copy of *Meccano Magazine*.

pp. 111–14 From contemporary postcards, publishers unknown, courtesy of Keith Towel.

p. 115 From a postcard published by Raphael Tuck.

p. 116 Kevan from London, England, CC BY 2.0, via Wikimedia Commons.

p. 118 Courtesy of James Styles.

p. 119 From a postcard published by Valentine.

p. 129 Anthony Harrison and Clive Warneford, via Wikimedia Commons.

p. 130 Courtesy of Bill Hodgson and Phil Bennett.

pp. 136, 139 First published by BFR Publications in *Coronation Pictures* souvenir brochure.

p. 143 Courtesy of pastposters.com.

p. 144 From a contemporary postcard.

p. 146 Courtesy of the Woolworths Museum (www.woolworthsmuseum.co.uk) © 3D and 6D pictures Ltd.

pp. 148–9 Courtesy of the Memorabilia Pack Company.

p. 151 Ministry of Information Photo Division Photographer, via Wikimedia Commons.

p. 152 Courtesy of the Memorabilia Pack Company.

p. 154 Courtesy of Ron Holloway.

pp. 159–61 Courtesy of the Woolworths Museum (www.woolworthsmuseum.co.uk) © 3D and 6D pictures Ltd.

p. 163 Courtesy of the Harpenden & District Local History Society.

p. 164 OSU Special Collections & Archives, via Wikimedia Commons.

p. 171 From a contemporary postcard.

p. 172 By Wouter Hagens, public domain, via Wikimedia Commons.

pp. 174–6 Courtesy of James W. Howie, Dundee.

p. 177 Courtesy of www.thegoonshow.net.

p. 178 © ABC Television.

p. 180 Courtesy of James W. Howie, Dundee.

p. 182 From a contemporary publicity picture, courtesy of Colosseum Autographs.

pp. 183–4 Courtesy of James W. Howie, Dundee.

p. 188 From the BBC Photo Library.

pp. 190–1 Courtesy of James W. Howie, Dundee.

p. 197 Courtesy of the Memorabilia Pack Company.

p. 203 Courtesy of Flints Auctions.

p. 205 From the BBC Photo Library.

p. 214 (top) From a contemporary postcard.

p. 214 (lower) Ministry of Information Photo Division Photographer, via Wikimedia Commons.

p. 216 Jhsteel, CC BY-SA 4.0, via Wikimedia Commons.

p. 222 Paramount Pictures artist, Public domain, via Wikimedia Commons.

p. 223 Copyrighted by Loew's International. Artists(s) not known, via Wikimedia Commons.

p. 225 Copyright 1954, Loew's Incorporated, via Wikimedia Commons.

p. 228 Reynold Brown, via Wikimedia Commons.

p. 230 (lower) 35mm scan by Chemical Engineer, via Wikimedia Commons.

p. 223 Courtesy of Pat Rowley.

p. 234 Courtesy of Peter Hampson.

p. 236 Arpingstone, via Wikimedia Commons.

p. 237 (top) Redsimon, via Wikimedia Commons.

p. 237 (lower) Courtesy of Morse Classics.

p. 239 Courtesy of Morse Classics.

p. 240 DeFacto, CC BY-SA 2.5, via Wikimedia Commons.

p. 245 (top) Richard Corfield, CC BY 2.0, via Wikimedia Commons.

p. 245 (lower) Public domain, via Wikimedia Commons.

p. 246 From a contemporary postcard.

p. 248 (top) Image edited by Shoepepper, CC BY 2.0, via Wikimedia Commons.

p. 248 (lower) Les Chatfield, CC BY 2.0, via Wikimedia Commons.

p. 251 Au Morandarte, CC BY-SA 2.0, via Wikimedia Commons.

p. 252 © Steve Beamish.

pp. 254–5 © Steve Beamish.

pp. 257–8 © Robert Darlaston.

p. 260 Ben Brooksbank, CC BY-SA 2.0, via Wikimedia Commons.

p. 261 From the collections of the Imperial War Museums.

p. 262 Scandinavian Airlines, via Wikimedia Commons.

Index